MODERN AIRCRAFT ⊲ W9-CXD-755

Edited by Joe Christy

A new series of popular-priced books on aircraft and their operation for everyone interested in privately owned planes. Each volume is written by an expert in the field, and is printed on fine, white paper and profusely illustrated with photographs and diagrams.

Learning to Fly

Your Pilot's License
Your FAA Flight Exam
Legal Guide for Pilots & Owners
Your Jet Pilot Rating
Airmanship After Solo
Pilot's Digest of FAA Regulations

Navigation and Weather

Nav/Com Guide for Pilots
Cockpit Navigation Guide
Pilot's Weather Guide
Air Traffic Control
Instrument Flying Guide
Computer Guide

Classics and Classes

Classic Biplanes
Classic Military Biplanes
Classic Monoplanes
Racing Planes Guide

Vocations and Avocations

Agricultural Aviation
Taking Pictures from the Air
How to Draw Airplanes
Jet Aircraft Engines

Individual Light Planes

Multiengine Flying
The Single-Engine Cessnas
The Piper Cub Story
The Single-Engine Beechcrafts
All About Helicopters

Flying Sports

Skysurfing
Hot Air Ballooning
Parachuting for Sport
Soaring Guide
Modern Aerobatics
Club Flying

Military Light Planes

Aces & Planes of WWI
The Curtiss Hawk Fighters
Scramble, British Aircraft WWII
Aircraft Armament

For the Home Builder

Guide to Homebuilts
Used Plane Buying Guide
Aircraft Dope & Fabric
Lightplane Construction &
  Repair
Custom Lightplane Design
Modern Lightplane Engines

Published by
SPORTS CAR PRESS

Distributed by Crown Publishers
419 Park Avenue South, New York, N.Y. 10016

Dedication

To the safety of the sport of skysurfing with hope it contributes in the prevention of accidents.

Skysurfing

a guide to hang gliding
Eddie Paul

New York

MODERN AIRCRAFT SERIES

A Division of Sports Car Press

Acknowledgment

For their help, I would like to thank Don Downie, Don Dwiggins, Bill Allen, Bill Bennett, Joe Faust, Irv Culver, and a special thanks to my wife, Kris.

© 1975 by Sports Car Press, Ltd.
Published in New York by Sports Car Press, Ltd.
and simultaneously in Ontario, Canada, by General
Publishing Co.

Manufactured in the U.S.A.

Produced by Silvermine Productions, Norwalk,
Connecticut 06850

LCCN 74-25883

ISBN 0-87112-069-0

CONTENTS

Hang gliders at Torrey Pines, California, an advanced ridge soaring site for experienced skysurfers. Record flights lasting hours have been set here. Photo by Downie and Associates.

1. What is Skysurfing?

Skysurfing has managed to capture the imagination of many due mainly to the fact that it is an equal opportunity sport in which old and young, rich and poor, men and women all start equal, all consuming equal amounts of sand on their first flights.

Skysurfing — or hang gliding — is one of the easiest sports to learn. All you need is a glider (nicknamed a "kite"), a hill, some wind and a few hours of training and you can call yourself a Skysurfer. I have seen people who have never flown anything before hop in a kite, listen to about five minutes of instruction and proceed to make what appeared to be a very experienced take-off, flight, and landing. I don't recommend it but it has happened.

Unlike many other sports, you need not be a Charles Atlas. You only need enough strength to assemble a glider and carry it up a hill — with the assistance of the wind. You then have to strap in, and run hard for a few dozen feet. Then you get to sit in your swing seat and look down on the rest of the world while you float effortlessly. Of course, if this appears to be too strenuous, most hang glider sites offer rides to the top of the hill.

Cost of the Sport

On the financial end of the sport, I have found that you can pay whatever you want. You can buy plans for about five dollars and build your own glider, saving the cost of labor. A friend of mine paid $210 for materials, put in one week of spare time, and had a kite equal to some of the $600 kites. And he has the knowledge of the construction of his kite. You can also pick up used kites for as little as $150 on up to $400. Or, if you want a new kite, you can find a few friends to chip in on one and cut your purchase cost. I think you will find that no matter how you get a kite, it will wind up being a low cost sport as compared to other sports. A few years ago, a friend and I built two kites on a very low budget of about $75 each and flew them everyday that summer for a total cost of $5.00 for a broken kingpost. Of course, costs have risen, but you can still get by for less than you can in most sports.

Another attractive feature to hang gliding is that in an ecology-oriented age it is a noiseless, pollution-free sport, so it fits our "concerned" society by offending few. Other advantages include easy portability, no age limitations, and no license requirements. Now you can see why skysurfing is one of the fastest growing sports today.

How it Works
Skysurfing is still a relatively new sport. It truly started sometime in 1971 and rapidly gained in popularity. It started with 10 to 20 people and by 1974 had well over 10,000 people involved with some 6,000 pilots flying every week.

The Rogallo wing, by far the most common surfing design because of its simplicity and low cost, was a hybrid designed by Francis M. Rogallo for N.A.S.A. and in essence it is nothing more than a flying parachute. It has about a four-to-one glide ratio which means if you fly off a 100-foot hill, you should glide forward about 400 feet in no wind.

N.A.S.A. found that by using a Rogallo wing as a lifting device, a helicopter could tow it behind with a load of over twice what it could lift without the Rogallo. N.A.S.A. also found that with flexible sail design, a man could jump out of a plane, pop his chute, and pin-point a landing some distance away by pulling on the suspension lines to warp the shape of the wing.

And so the main control of a Rogallo is achieved by weight shift. For example, in a hang glider, if you want to dive, you pull your weight forward, decreasing your angle of attack. If you want to climb, you push your weight back to increase your angle of attack in relation to the center of gravity (the center of gravity is you). To turn, you pull to the right to turn right; pull your weight to the left to turn left. The control is the same as for the paper planes you made as a child. If you wanted the plane to dive, you would add a paper clip to the nose and thus be moving the center of gravity forward to achieve more speed which also increases the stability.

However, weight shift does have its limitations, which are extreme angles of attack in which the glider becomes less responsive to weight shift. Extreme dives, stalls, and turns should be avoided.

The Reason Why
There is something about the experience of hang gliding that is

Good form, good flight by an expert flyer using a standard Rogallo wing. But he should be wearing a helmet!

hard to express to those who have never tried it. It's like describing color to a blind man. Where do you start? And so most people start, just as I have, by telling you how cheap it is, how easy it is, and how much fun it is. But that's where it ends because it is hard to describe the feeling one gets from skysurfing. It seems odd but most pilots don't seem to know what it is that makes them want to spend hours carrying 40 lbs. of aluminum and Dacron up a mountainside for the few brief minutes it takes to fly gracefully to the bottom.

I can remember when I first got into the sport it reminded me of the times when I would jump off sand dunes as a kid. One day someone came up and asked why I spent all that time climbing up the sand dune just to jump off. I didn't have an answer then and I don't have one now.

I've tried to think of something to relate hang gliding to but came up with nothing except that all our lives we are told to avoid high places. We build up a fear of height. Then one day you are sitting in a toy swing seat, apparently suspended by a rope smaller than your little finger, 300 feet above a crowded beach. You hear nothing but the wind, you feel no movement. It's as if you are hanging on some invisible line suspended from heaven. You can just sit in one spot looking down on rooftops, people, and telephone poles. For the first time in your life you may see what the top of a seagull looks like as he soars below you. You can turn, dive, climb or ridge soar; but just sitting in one spot hovering and looking down on the people is to me an ultimate thrill because I don't feel I am flying but floating. No matter how long you hang glide, it is hard to get used to this hovering mode because even though you have sufficient wind speed to fly, you have no ground speed. It's hard to convince your mind that when something is standing still it is still flying.

The Easy Appeal
What attracts most people to hang gliding is its simplicity. For instance, in how many sports can a 14-year-old boy become proficient with about three weeks experience? I have seen pilots fly while wearing stereo headphones or playing a harmonica. I have even heard of one young pilot who is installing a portable television on his control bar so he can watch it while trying to set a new endurance record.

Which brings us to a major aspect of hang gliding. Most people have the misconception that you carry your kite up a hill, jump off and fly down. This is the case with the beginner. But there is much

Modern skysurfing includes the flexible, Rogallo-type wings and efficient, sophisticated, rigid wing designs. This VJ-23 Swingwing is probably the highest efficiency hang glider in the world. It was built and is flown here by Volmer Jensen, 63-year-old Californian who was building hang gliders 40 years ago! Photo by Downie and Associates.

more to skysurfing and it is called soaring. As you become more proficient, you learn that by turning about 45 degrees to some hills, you can stay in the high lift area and soar for extended periods.

For example, there is a small sand dune in Los Angeles known as Playa del Rey. It's 20 feet from top to bottom and about 1,000 feet long. Usually, a nice strong ocean breeze is blowing straight into it. It's used as a training site with flights of about three seconds common for beginners. After flying there for two years, I found the lift areas and memorized them so that I once stayed up for five minutes in a 15 m.p.h. wind. At the time I weighed 220 pounds and was flying a 16-foot Porta-Wing. So you can see that with experience you can soar even a 20-foot sand dune with ease. With a 50-foot sand dune and a 15 m.p.h. wind, you might soar for hours.

Learn to Be Low
Another point to keep in mind while learning to fly is to stay low and, if possible, to stay over sand. Become as proficient as possible at lower altitudes before going to higher hills because no matter how high your take-off, eventually you have to enter low altitude winds and you should know what to expect. Many a pilot has made a beautiful flight from a high hill, then misjudged his landing speed, and bashed his knuckles on the ground.

Keep in mind that if you stall in the air, you can recover by diving a little to pick up speed. But if you stall near the ground, you can't dive. You should keep your airspeed up. This can only be done by knowing how fast you are going. Since kites don't have airspeed indicators, the only way to know your speed is by experience. You can't depend on waiting for your sail to luff to give you an indication of your speed because with most of the new-design hang gliders, the sails won't luff until after you have stalled. You have to acquire a feel for knowing your speed. This is not as hard as it sounds.

Hearing, Balance and Gorillas
A big hang glider company once sold helmets with ear cutouts with the claim that you need to "hear" the wind to know how fast you are going. This sold a lot of helmets, but I have found that you don't need to hear the wind. The way I found out was when we decided that the cover of our next issue of Man-Flight magazine needed a gorilla flying a kite. This may sound simple enough unless you were there. To begin with, it was midsummer outside the gorilla suit and even hotter inside. We decided that a gorilla would look out-of-place in a swing seat or a harness. He should fly while standing on

the control bar, because that's the way gorillas fly.

After donning the 30-pound ape suit, I discovered a slight problem (not to mention my gross weight of 250 pounds). I couldn't feel, see or hear. However, if I turned my head sideways I could see through the ear, so there was still the possibility of doing it. To my amazement, I found that without the senses of touch, hearing, and sight, my flights were as good as they were without the suit. I came to the conclusion that we use our sense of balance for control which, when combined with weight-shift control, comes to be as natural as walking. So, you might want to get a helmet with more ear protection. Obviously, alcoholic drinks or drugs that affect the sense of balance should be strenuously avoided by hang glider flyers.

Illusions and Conclusions

Another thing to remember is not to rely on sight to determine your airspeed. Even if you are correct at low altitudes, at higher altitudes you will have the feeling that you are stalling and you will have a tendency to dive to pick up some speed when in reality you are going too fast already. This is known as divers' syndrome. It's just like a car passing you at 50 m.p.h. 10 feet away. It looks like it is going faster than a car 100 feet away doing 60 m.p.h. It is necessary to memorize your position in relation to the control bar and try to maintain that position when flying at higher altitudes.

This introduction includes some spare thoughts about the basics of hang gliding. The following chapters go into more depth. However, when you buy a kite, always talk to the manufacturer about its handling characteristics. If he says things which contradict what you read in this book, you should do as he suggests. Every kite is different. They have different characteristics which make them as individual as airplanes. This book is not describing all kites, but the basic principles of hang gliding and the general characteristics of kites I know. There are many high-performance kites on the market which require specialized training. You should learn this from the recommended schools. If you do this and don't get over-confident — the biggest problem in the sport — you can expect to have many fun-filled years of flying, not to mention being a pioneer in the new and rapidly growing sport *Skysurfing!*

2. History of Powerless Flight

Hang gliding or skysurfing is by no stretch of the imagination a new sport. It is probably one of the oldest sports, second only to dinosaur races.

The sport probably started when early man first glanced skyward and asked himself, "Why not?" From that day forth, man has attempted to defy the law of gravity. With every combination of materials available to him, man's imagination ran wild with designs. The first designs look like birds or bats. Slowly they took on the configuration we now refer to as the glider or airplane.

Flight was discovered, it seems, by the process of elimination. Find the designs that won't fly and the remaining designs must fly. Man was tormented by the invisible wall or barrier that seemed to separate him from the birds and insects. It must have seemed odd to early man that the greatest heroes with the best designs and equipment could do little more than flap into total exhaustion with the new wings fashioned from bits of wood, string, and cloth — while bugs flew with irritating ease!

Being stubborn, man continued his fight for flight and, often believed the mystery of flight to be solved. So, with wings on their backs men began leaping from very high towers and these early aviators became historic fatalities with each jump. These early "Tower Jumpers" such as the Flying Saracen, who made an exhibition annihilation jump before King Comenus, caused very serious consideration of the problems of flight.

Leonardo da Vinci (1452-1519) spent weeks observing birds in flight. He sketched designs for his own flying machine which his assistant Zoroastro was contracted to build from Leonardo's drawings and instructions. History reveals that this design was tried by its designer and due to low structural integrity and heavy wing loading it collapsed.

Not being one to give up easily, Leonardo started a new design which would include a tail. Whether it would act as an elevator is not known but it would serve as a stabilizer for the new wing which Zoroastro had completed. For days Leonardo tried tail designs of

In 1175 the "Flying Saracen," an early tower jumper, leaped off a high tower and went down in history as the "Falling Saracen."

The first living passengers in September of 1783 were a rooster, a duck, and a sheep taken aloft in Joseph and Etienne Montgolfier's balloon.

which none satisfied him. Knowing that he had other work, he abandoned the flying machine and instructed Zoroastro to do likewise. This was not unusual for Leonardo. He would jump from one project to another and often come back with a fresh approach. Not being a man of such patience and having faith in anything that Leo-

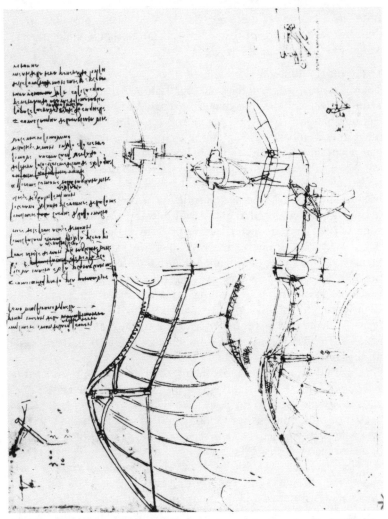

Leonardo showed little more than a passing curiosity in flight. But during those few weeks, he discovered more than others had discovered in thousands of years. Photo by Don Dwiggins.

nardo designed, Zoroastro waited until Leonardo left home. He then attempted to be the first pilot of a flying wing. He was! But like so many before him, he never flew again and was crippled for life.

This was followed by many bizarre attempts at flight such as

Besnier's Flapping Vanes in 1678. None of these provided more than brief entertainment to the few spectators that would gather to watch the futile attempts at flight.

Montgolfiers' Balloon

Then it happened. On September 19, 1783, Joseph and Etienne Montgolfier sent the first living passengers to an altitude of 1500 feet in a balloon. The flyers were a rooster, a duck and a sheep, and they landed unharmed, something that up to this time only birds had accomplished. And so the balloon was to be the center of almost every flying machine design from 1783 to the late 1800's when a German engineer named Otto Lilienthal and his brother Gustav became immersed in the basic problems of flight.

Lilienthal recognized the superior lifting qualities of a curved wing with a large diameter leading edge over that of the flat plate wing. With the principle established to his satisfaction, both by theory and then by experiment, Lilienthal stated in 1889, "We also find that nature utilizes the advantage of curved wings even in the vegetable kingdom, by providing the seeds of certain plants with slightly curved wings, so as to enable them to sail along in the wind." Lilienthal was probably referring to the leaf of the Zanonia Macrocarpa which carries a seed and has washout tips. It will glide up to five miles.

Lilienthal decided to put his theory to practice. The results led to a series of gliders with rigid wings, first on monoplane gliders (single wings) and later to biplanes (two wings).

He not only built his own gliders, but he also built the hill from which he flew his gliders. It is reported that from this 50-foot hill, he made many of his 2,000 flights.

Lilienthal used the same type of control many of today's hang gliders use. Weight shift! He reported that after a while his moves became so instinctive and automatic he felt at home in the air.

On August 9, 1896, while testing a glider that he planned to power soon by a carbonic-acid motor, he lost control and plunged to the ground 50 feet below. Otto Lilienthal died that day, but in his 48 years of life he managed to turn flight from a dream to a reality. In his life, he managed to do things no other man had done. He achieved flights up to a quarter of a mile in distance at heights up to 75 feet and all on a craft utilizing only weight shift for control. Perhaps most important, by his accomplishments he aroused widespread enthusiasm among others interested in flight.

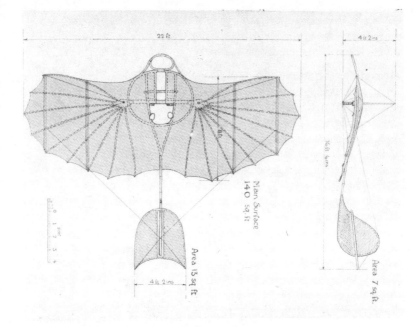

Basic dimensions of Lilienthal's glider.

Other Pioneers

On September 30, 1899, Percy S. Pilcher, a young Englishman, had promised to give a gliding demonstration. After one attempt, the tow rope leading to horses broke. On a second try, he managed to rise to a height of 30 feet when a flying wire snapped and the machine crashed. Pilcher died the next day from his injuries.

John J. Montgomery of Santa Clara, California, started building ornithopters in 1883, but the flight results, if any, are uncertain. More certain is the fact that Montgomery built several man-carrying gliders which he launched from balloons. One of Montgomery's test pilots, Dan Maloney, launched from a balloon at a height of 4,000 feet. He demonstrated quite remarkable control, including a corkscrew and side somersaults. Maloney's flying ended in 1908 in a fatal crash.

Montgomery later built his last and best glider, the Evergreen. Glides of nine minutes were reported. During a low-speed stall and crash, Montgomery was thrown against the frame. His head struck a bolt and he died.

In 1896 and 1897, Octave Chanute made some 2,000 gliding

On a good day, in a good wind, the Wrights managed to soar on the sand slopes of Kitty Hawk. Note the sand bag on nose for balance. Below, even the Wright Brothers had bad days. Photos courtesy Hatfield History of Aeronautics.

Otto Lilienthal stands atop the hill he built for testing his designs. He could take off in any direction from this hill and he did some 2,000 times. Photos courtesy Hatfield History of Aeronautics. Drawings, below, show first and second hill built by Lilienthal for the purpose of testing his hang gliders. First hill is shown at bottom. He later doubled the size of his hill and achieved more spectacular results as shown by dotted lines representing his glide path. Note his storage lofts where he housed 4 to 6 gliders when not in use!

flights along the shores of Lake Michigan. Chanute's gliders differed from Lilienthal's in one important respect. Where Lilienthal sought to maintain stability during flight by shifting his body weight, Chanute proposed a mechanism that would move the wings to control stability.

Chanute invited "other experiments to improve upon our practice" in 1897. In March of 1900, Wilbur Wright answered his invitation and the interchange of letters marked the beginning of a long and lasting friendship between Octave Chanute and Wilbur and Orville Wright. Some even believe that Chanute might have seen the first successful flight. The Wrights gained much from Chanute in guidance as Chanute gained much from the Wrights in pride.

Dan Maloney at controls with John J. Montgomery at far right. This is the Santa Clara which was balloon launched from 4,000 feet 75 years ago. Courtesy Hatfield History of Aeronautics.

3. Flying a Hang Glider.

Flying a hang glider comes so naturally that most people are airborne within the first three jumps. They are not ready for snap rolls but they are actually flying by themselves. As a matter of fact, this is one bad aspect of hang gliding: it is so easy to learn that many people after one or two jumps want to go higher. If they are unassisted, they will often get into trouble. For that reason, you should have instruction from a qualified teacher (qualified on the brand of hang glider you have).

A qualified instructor is not always handy or may charge too much. So, you may want to learn by yourself. It is not impossible. I learned by myself and I think I learned more than anyone could have taught me because I found out what would happen when I did something wrong. When the kite was damaged I had to fix it, so I soon became very careful.

If you do decide to learn by yourself, I have found the following method to be the best. First, you need some equipment which should consist of a hang glider (in this case, a Rogallo); a crash helmet with face shield; wind meter; gloves, boots, heavy pants, heavy jacket; and a movie camera (Super 8 is fine). The camera is the best training tool you can use. Someone watching you can't see and remember everything that happens but, if you have a movie, you can play it and replay it to find out why you crashed or stalled or even why you made a perfect flight.

The next thing to bring with you is a friend. Hang gliding, like scuba diving, should never be practiced alone. The main reason is that if you get hurt you need help. Having a friend along may some day save your life.

Of course, your friend can operate the camera during your learning flights.

You also need a place to fly. This may seem easy but on your first flights you need a perfect spot. When you gain experience you will find yourself flying from some not-so-perfect spots. The perfect hill should be about 20 to 30 feet from top to bottom. It should have

Left, weight shift to control pitch of hang glider. Move body forward to dive, move body back to climb or stall. Right, weight shift to control heading of a hang glider. Move body in the direction you wish to turn.

a slope to match your glide angle, about 1 to 3. A 20-foot hill should have a base 60 feet from the take-off point.

The hill should have no rocks or obstacles of any kind. The ideal hill is a low sand dune facing a flat plain, ocean, or lake. The reason is that you can get undisturbed air coming up the slope. Last but not least, you should have a 10 m.p.h. steady wind coming straight at the slope toward you, not across the hill or down the hill.

Your First Assault

Now that you have your equipment and your perfect hill, you are ready to launch your personal assault against gravity. But first you must assemble your glider. This is best done at the top of the hill with the nose facing into the wind. The glider should have been assembled in no wind at home a few times before to become familiar with the process of assembly. If this was done, assembly in a wind should pose no big problem. Just the same, be careful to point the nose into the wind and keep the nose of the kite on the ground until you are ready to fly.

After the kite is assembled, walk around it and double check everything. If you are with a friend who also has a kite, check each

Prone flying position is by far the most spectacular but requires more movement for control. This is a special ski kite with flotation gear towed to launch behind a power boat.

other's gliders as well as each other's swing seats or harnesses. When satisfied, check the wind speed with your wind meter. If the wind is gusty or over 10 m.p.h., you shouldn't take a chance. On a low hill you will have a hard time hurting yourself, but you could very easily bust up your kite in a few seconds and could cause over $100 damage. So, it is not worth taking a chance when you are learning.

If the wind is good and you are ready to give it a try, your next step is to step toward the edge of the hill. Hold the control bar with both hands and use your elbows against the back of the control bar down tubes to keep the kite in a neutral position to diminish the drag. This will allow you to gain more speed for the take-off.

The Life Mode
Now, slowly relax your elbow pressure allowing the nose to tilt up until you see the sail fill with air. It is now in a lift mode. This will later be done to take off and to flare. You may notice the wing wanting to lift more on one side than the other. If so, this indicates the wind is coming from that one side. By pointing the nose toward the high wing, that wing will drop to a level position. Try this deliberately to familiarize yourself with your hang glider.

When you feel you have control of your wing, position yourself about 10 feet behind the top of the hill, facing into the wind and

Champion flyer Bob Wills with a pupil in his unusual two-person glider.

holding the kite in the neutral position. If a friend is helping to launch you, he should be instructed as follows: If you have a lousy launch, you have a lousy flight.

The person at the end of your keel is as important as the person at the control bar, so let him know it is important he be alert. He is to hold the keel at the proper height to allow the angle of attack of the kite to be at zero, or so the sail is completely luffing (neither positive nor negative). He should know the basics of flying because if you get a bad start the tail launcher can lever the nose into the proper position to keep you flying. Finally, the tail launcher should never shove the keel or hold it tightly. He is only there to assist in control for take-off. If he does shove, you will get used to this extra power for take-off and not be able to fly without it. As soon as you can fly without a tail launcher, do so!

Run to Fly
If you are self launching, holding the kite in the neutral position,

start a fast run toward the edge of the hill maintaining the kite in the neutral position. As you approach the edge of the hill, you will feel the kite lift and you should start to push out on the control bar and this in turn will start the kite climbing. As you feel the kite lift, you will be lifted off the ground. Pull back slightly on the control bar to gain some flying speed and to get your glide angle. Now, as you approach the ground, push out on the control bar slightly to slow down and pull out of the glide.

While learning, remember that on small hills it is safer to stall than to dive! So, "When in doubt, push out!"

Now that you have completed your first flight, you should practice this over and over until you can take off unassisted and land on your feet every time.

You can now learn to turn. Although turning is simple, most people have problems with it. All you have to do is pull your body the way you want to go.

For example, if you want to go right, pull your body to the right. If you want to turn left, pull your body to the left. People get confused about what part of the body to pull left or right. Some people tilt the top of their body to the right and expect the kite to turn right. To their dismay, they proceed to glide straight ahead and grumbling about their uncontrollable glider. What they did not see was that while the top of their body leaned to the right, their legs went to the left, which counteracted the well-intended turn.

Other things to watch out for in turns include inadvertently twisting your body while turning. Keep your feet together and don't lean. Always sit straight up and down and pull your whole body over to one side and your kite will turn. Always keep your speed up in a turn by pulling your body forward a little before a turn. While learning to fly, the camera is a very helpful item to find out what you are doing right or wrong, especially during this turning phase.

Stay Low and Practice!
You are now approaching the second most dangerous feeling in a skysurfer's life. (The most dangerous being an experienced pilot's overconfidence.) You will soon feel that you are the hottest pilot in the sky and you will want to start high altitude jumps. It happens to everyone. It will happen to you, so remember this if you can. A friend of mine got involved in hang gliding and learned very quickly. He soon got the urge to increase his take-off altitude at an alarming rate. He went to a 100-foot cliff and then to a 500-foot hill in very bad wind conditions. After take-off, he turned downwind and

Sequence taken by Dana Downey of her father's first attempt at skysurfing. 1. A fast run into a five mph wind. 2. Airborne and probably wondering what he's doing here. 3. Final approach pattern. 4. Touchdown to all points landing. 5. Trying to think of a good explanation to give the F.A.A. for landing without permission.

stalled. Not having much experience, he pushed out thinking he was in a dive because of his fast ground speed. He then stalled in at about·35 m.p.h. and spent about three months in the hospital. It could have been avoided with about one more week of practice and training.

So, I can't stress the point enough about learning to fly by lots of low altitude practice. You don't need a license, so you have no test to pass. However, in a test, you get a second chance. In a hang glider you sometimes don't. Have some respect for your glider and, if you get confident in your flying ability, stop flying for a while and

① FACE WIND, LIFT NOSE TO FILL SAIL.
② RUN INTO WIND WITH NOSE UP (AS SHOWN)
③ AS SOON AS YOU LEAVE THE GROUND, PULL
   BACK ON CONTROL BAR A LITTLE.
④ KEEP A GOOD GLIDE ANGLE (DRAWING AT LEFT
   IS EXAGGERATED)
⑤ IF YOU DIVE (AS SHOWN) YOU WILL GAIN SPEED.
⑥ TO LAND PUSH HARD ON CONTROL BAR TO STALL
   AND YOU SHOULD LAND AT ZERO M.P.H.
⑦ AFTER YOU LAND POINT NOSE INTO WIND AND PUT NOSE
DOWN. THE WIND WILL HOLD YOUR "FLYING WING" FROM
MOVING.

A basic, straight-ahead hang-gliding flight.

start watching the newspaper for hang glider accidents. You will find that it is not a toy. It is an aircraft. Some of the overconfident, top-notch pilots who helped develop the sport are dead from some of the most basic mistakes.

4. Winds and Turbulence

"If you can't see it, it isn't there!" This seems to be the attitude of new pilots concerning winds and turbulence. However, as their experience increases their attitudes change to a total acceptance of the fact that, "If you can't see it, it can still be there!"

When the sport of hang gliding started, nobody seemed to know much about winds or the effect they had on a kite. So, we were learning by the trial-and-error method and we sometimes wound up with a scrap pile of aluminum tubes at the end of the day. For financial reasons, we decided to learn what was destroying our kites and kicking us around in the air.

We found that airplanes and sailplanes seldom run into the turbulence that a kite will hit because they are higher in the lift or air. A kite is close to the terrain and gets hit by every bump in the ground effects.

Understanding Air

A basic knowledge of meteorology (the study of the weather) is in order along with a basic knowledge of aerodynamics, the science of air in motion.

The best place to start is with "A" which stands for air. Air is a blanket of gases (mostly nitrogen and oxygen) which surrounds the earth. Like any gas, it is readily displaced at the slightest provocation — by a moving object, by heat or by cold. Air has weight as any scuba diver can attest after having a tank filled. And it also has density which is affected by pressure, temperature and humidity. Air density decreases with height. For example: The density of air at an altitude of 320,000 feet is 1/1,000.000th of the density at sea level.

Even though it seems that science knows everything there is to know about air and its effect on objects, there is still confusion between theory and observation.

Much of the confusion stems from the fact that air is invisible, causing a hindrance to observation. Fortunately, there are ways of

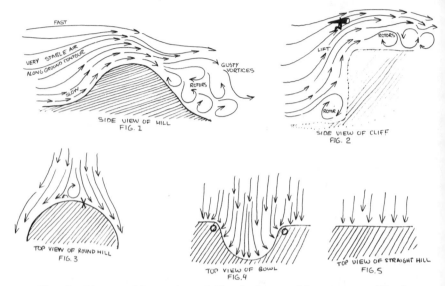

Fig. 1: Above a dome-type hill, wind speed increases with altitude and a hang glider can be blown over the hill into the gusty and dangerous wind rotors on the leeward side.

Fig. 2: Cliff or ridge soaring is for the proficient as the ultimate form of skysurfing. Lift and rotor areas along a sharp cliff are quite predictable but the flying technique is very specialized and different from that used when flying into a wind blowing horizontally.

Fig. 3: A round top hill will have strong wind deflections and it is important to take off near the "center" marked X where the wind is likely to be coming at the smallest angle.

Fig. 4: The most unpredictable wind currents around a bowl are likely to be at the points marked with small circles.

Fig. 5: The most predictable winds are at 90 degrees against the face of a straight hill.

making the air visible for study. One is the use of tufts of wool to indicate air flow over a wing or other surface. Other ways include injecting a foreign substance into the air flow upwind of an object to see the flow past the object. Many facts have been learned by such tests, facts which apply to hang gliders as well as to aircraft.

Since hang gliders utilize gravity for power through the air, and they have no motor to help them get out of a bad situation, there are more air restrictions applying to the skysurfer than to the pilot of an airplane. One main rule is: Adverse weather conditions should be avoided like the plague.

Ridge Lift and Thermal Lift

Most of the lift encountered by the skysurfer is ridge lift and not thermal lift as thought by many. Ridge lift is the upward flow of

Fig. 6: The turbulence arrows indicate why you should never fly a hill (number 2) with another, similar hill (number 1) upwind of you.

Fig. 7: Wind through a pass can be smooth and fast but soon becomes slow and turbulent.

Fig. 8: Air flowing past an obstacle reacts much the same as an obstacle passing through the air. Visualize water passing by a rock in a stream.

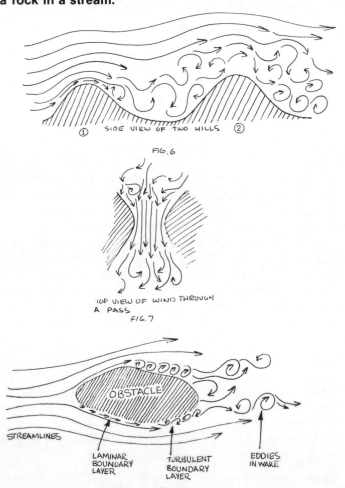

① SIDE VIEW OF TWO HILLS ②

FIG. 6

TOP VIEW OF WIND THROUGH A PASS

FIG. 7

STREAMLINES

OBSTACLE

LAMINAR BOUNDARY LAYER

TURBULENT BOUNDARY LAYER

EDDIES IN WAKE

FIG 8

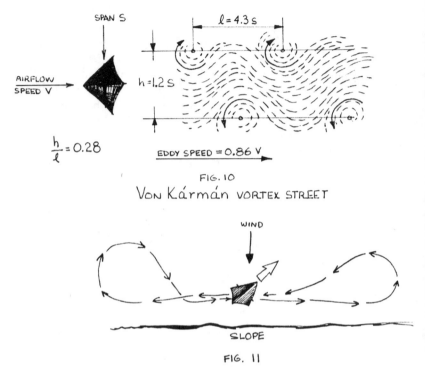

SPAN S

AIRFLOW SPEED V

$\ell = 4.3\,s$

$h = 1.2\,s$

$\dfrac{h}{\ell} = 0.28$

EDDY SPEED $= 0.86\,V$

FIG. 10

Von Kármán VORTEX STREET

WIND

SLOPE

FIG. 11

Fig. 10: A hang glider moving from right to left produces a wake in its passage. The very turbulent wake is dangerous to another hang glider following too closely behind.

Fig. 11: Slope, ridge or cliff soaring is specialized and only for advanced flyers. The ideal flight path shown is achieved by flying at a "crabbed" heading slightly into the wind in the direction of travel. Turns are always made away from the hill. The direction of the wind is at 90 degrees to the ridge line but the wind rushes up the slope nearly vertically creating lift and the opportunity for extended flight.

air caused by a hill or cliff. It is the main lift used by the skysurfer for a number of reasons. A new pilot can find ridge lift with little knowledge of wind flow. It offers a dependable and strong lift in a very wide zone (depending on size and shape of the hill, of course) and it can be found in the same location as long as the wind is coming from the same direction. It can be found knowing nothing more than wind direction.

Thermals, on the other hand, are rarely used by the low efficiency Rogallos but are used by the high efficiency gliders such as Taras Kiceniuk's Icarus V. A knowledge of thermals is still necessary for conventional hang glider pilots. The mechanics of a thermal are simple. The prediction of a thermal is not so simple. Man-made thermals can be seen in everyday life, such as smoke coming out of a chimney or steam coming out of a pan of boiling water. Man-made thermals are usually a by-product of something else, although someday it may be the main product. A thermal lift center with predicted thermal release times may someday be located at areas with no ridge lift. It may sound far out, but then 10 years ago skysurfing sounded far out.

Thermals are not seasonal. They can pop up at any location or time whenever there is an uneven ground temperature. They are most commonly found over dark areas (black absorbs heat while white reflects heat) like parking lots, plowed ground, or dark rocks. For example: If you have a white area with a ten-foot black dot in the center, the white area will be reflecting the sun's rays while the black area absorbs. When it has absorbed enough heat the black area will allow a bubble of this heated air to rise (heat rises and cool air settles) thus creating a thermal which can extend up thousands of feet.

Two other types of lift are wave lift and frontal lift. Neither type is for the novice and should only be attempted by the very experienced pilot.

The illustrations should help you understand wind flow and turbulence or at least get a basic familiarity of them. It would be impossible to explain wind flow completely because there is still much unknown about it. So, in a manner of speaking, you are on a new frontier which has been bypassed during man's quest for power. It is a frontier that has only been touched by man and may lead to a new future in which noise does not exist.

5. Safety is You!

How dangerous is hang gliding? Two years ago the answer would have been something like, "As safe as riding a bicycle." At that time skysurfers followed the golden rule. Never fly higher than you care to fall! Death was unheard of and injury rare.

As time marched on the golden rule was held inadequate and un-related to the "new" sport of skysurfing. People started leaping off higher and higher hills with less and less experience. One person was teaching people to fly off a 100-foot cliff with the old sink-or-swim attitude. Needless to say, death and destruction crept into the sport. Accidents became a common occurrence with the "growth of the sport" taking the blame.

But what about the old golden rule of skysurfing, you might ask? Well, it has been revised to, "There is safety in altitude." And the one I always liked, "Altitude is your friend." This all sounds fine if you are in an airplane; but in a hang glider suspended by two straps with only weight shift for control, I feel the old golden rule still applies!

I have not always felt this way, as many people know. There was a very deciding incident in my life due to an unexpected assault against Mother Nature in which I lost. However, I did manage to rearrange the molecular structure of a small portion of Mrs. Peggy Dahl's real estate, making it all seem almost worthwhile.

Like a Bad Movie

It seems like a bad movie, when I look back at it, one of these movies you advise your friends not to see. You always think that it's not going to happen to you. You try to figure out why God doesn't like you anymore. "Was it something that I said?"

Anyway, my injustice was dealt to me at Torrance Beach, Cali-fornia. After two very successful flights in some very gusty winds, I attempted a third. I found the wind had increased to 40 m.p.h. and was still very gusty but, after all, I had been flying for two years and never been hurt. Why start to worry now? I finally managed to get to the top of Torrance and watched the two pilots in front of me crash, making a total of 18 crashes in less than two hours.

Yours truly, breaking every rule in the book — flying higher than I cared to fall, flying in high winds (40 M.P.H.), and flying in gusty winds.

I started to have second thoughts when someone yelled, "You're next!" How could I back out now? Everyone would put me down and say my kite was no good. When you are a manufacturer you can't back down or your product is attacked.

So, I took a deep breath, had some boy hold my front wires while I collected my nerve, then when I figured I could stall no longer, I yelled, "O.K.!" and he let go of my front wire.

The kite lifted faster than it had ever done before. About five seconds later I was looking down one hundred feet at my take-off spot. I leaned about two inches to the left and the kite started a real nice banking turn. I began to relax a little and enjoy the ride. I went about as far south as I could without gaining too much altitude. I then proceeded to turn and make my flight north along the ridge.

As I approached the take-off area, I looked for a good spot to turn around. The wind was coming from the southwest and creating a lot of rough spots in the air as I was trying to turn. I had just en-

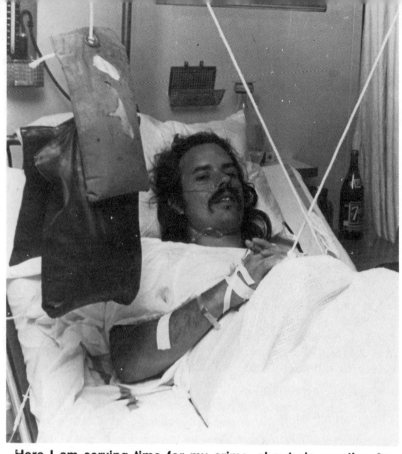

Here I am serving time for my crime, about six months. At least I learned my lesson. I have only flown low hills since.

tered a strong sink area so I turned into it and leaned into the prone position to gain speed. My altitude was about two hundred feet at this point. I dove for what seemed like hours but was only about three seconds. The rest took about two seconds but seemed like more hours.

Wind Blows Down, Too!

I can remember while diving thinking about the recent accidents in which pilots couldn't pull out of dives. In fact, the day before I saw a standard Rogallo nose in with the pilot completely prone and pushed out. Luckily, he only broke his shoulder. His kite had shown no response to his actions because he had hit a sink area and couldn't get up enough flying speed.

After about two Kung Fu flashbacks, I decided I did not want to become a statistic, so I pushed out hard expecting to hit the ground, while displaying fantastic form if nothing else. I remember suddenly feeling intense pain in my stomach, the type of pain you would expect if you dove 50 feet into a swimming pool and you did a belly flop. At first, I thought I hit the ground. But I could still feel the wind. But it was coming in a different direction. It was coming up. Looking down, I found that my flight was not yet terminated. I was now falling from about 50 feet.

I don't know why but it didn't scare me. I guess I didn't have time to be scared. Instead, I was planning my new landing. I was thinking, "Land feet first and you won't get hurt. Bend your knees and try to relax."

It must have worked. I came to after about five minutes and found myself two feet away from a chain link fence. I didn't feel any pain and couldn't think of a good encore for the 300 people who had gathered around. I was thrown a barrage of questions. "Does it hurt?" "How old are you?" "What hospital do you want to go to?" I then lost my sense of humor. They can ask me all the dumb questions they want, stick all the needles they want in my arm; but they are not going to take me to any hospital.

Expensive Rule-breaking

Later that evening at Harbor General Hospital I found that I was hurt. I had about five organs hemorrhaging, a busted pelvis, two broken ribs, and a slight concussion. I don't remember the first week. My wife said I was delirious. I was in intensive care, then transferred to a regular room for one week. I got a blood clot on my left lung and was rushed back to intensive care with the sick people again.

After five weeks I had a lot of time to think. I read my last editorial in which I pushed safety and set down some good rules to fly by. I found I had broken every rule in the book. For this I was laid up for about six months and paid a $15,000 hospital bill. But at least I am around to talk about it.

We did manage to get a film of the complete flight including the crash. We have watched the film at least 100 times and found that in the dive I must have reached 50 m.p.h. at which point I pushed the kite into an accelerated stall. This took five frames of the film which was running through the camera at 24 frames per second. We have computed that I was pulling a modest 10 G's and with my weight at 220 pounds I put a load of over 2200 pounds on the kite at

This was his first flight off a 100-foot hill with almost no training. Given adequate training, this might never have happened.

Luckily he was all right. After inspecting the kite, it was found that the bottom wires were fastened by "U" bolts and gave way on impact.

this point. We assume the cross tube bent allowing the wings to fold together. I say, "We assumed" because the film shows a side view of the kite and it does not look like the wings folded. But common sense tells us that you can't pull 10 G's without something bending. The kite was in better shape than I was. It had two bent tubes, at each end of the cross tube, about four feet in from the end. We believe one was bent hitting the ground. No cables were damaged and the sail was undamaged.

It Can Happen to You

Looking back at the accident, I honestly feel that it was totally caused by ignoring some of the basic rules of skysurfing. Don't fly higher than you care to fall. Don't fly in gusty winds. Don't fly in high winds. Don't panic. Maybe what happened to me can help others realize it can happen to them. Most important of all, people should realize that a kite it not a toy. It can bring many hours of fun if used right. If used wrong, it can put you in an early grave. *It's Up to You!*

I worked out some rules to fly by while I was in the hospital and they may help you. First of all, "Never fly higher than you care to fall" puts people off because they think you can only jump from a five-foot hill and that's it. But what they don't understand is that the rule means don't let your altitude exceed a safe distance from the ground, say seven to ten feet. So you may fly over a mile in distance or you may ridge soar a 30-foot sand dune. With today's gliders this is entirely possible.

Never do stunt flying! As of late, there are a number of pilots doing stunts in hang gliders who are not leaving a lasting impression on anything except the ground. For example: One young boy (19) was attempting a "hang" (a term given to a position in which the pilot hangs by his knees from the control bar and expects applause from the crowd). It was reported that he must have caught a down gust and dove in from 500 feet to his death. Not more than five minutes later it was attempted by another pilot who only managed to break his back. You get an idea how hard it is to get the "no stunting" point across to people.

Do Not Lend

Another rule to remember is never lend your kite unless you know that the borrower has respect for your equipment and is a well-qualified pilot. Most people don't realize that lending a kite is like lending your car. If the person who borrows it gets hurt or hurts someone else, you can be held responsible. I have also heard of people lending kites which, after being returned, the owner found damaged. The borrower forgot to tell the owner about this. This could have cost the owner his life. Be sure and go through every part and check your kite before flying. Remember you are not lending out an old coat. You are lending a precision piece of equipment which your life will depend on every time you fly. So, it is imperative you know exactly the condition of your kite at all times. For example: If you land on a wing tip you would know that it is now weaker and that you should only fly near the ground until repaired.

Always wear a crash helmet. The best type is a full Bell helmet which offers face protection as well as ear protection. You may be told that you need a helmet design that permits you to hear the wind in your sail. It sounds good but I have found that you don't fly by sound, you fly by feel. If you don't believe it, next time you fly, stick some cotton in your ears and see if your flying is impaired. Get the best helmet money can buy because it will be less expensive than busting your head in a "cheap" helmet. You also want a good set of boots and gloves, as well as a thick pair of pants.

All this probably has you wondering how safe skysurfing really is. All I can say is that it is as safe as the person behind the control bar. If you are the type of person who wants a thrill and you don't care about rules, do yourself, as well as the sport, a favor and don't get involved in skysurfing. On the other hand, if you want the joy of flight and are willing to obey a few rules to the letter, it can be as safe as any other sport and your chances of injury are slight. So, it comes down to another old saying, "Obey the rules and fly, disobey the rules and die."

6. Designing and Constructing a Hang Glider

The best place to start when constructing a glider is with the frame or main structure. I will explain the construction of a Rogallo wing and not a monoplane. There are more than 20 times as many Rogallos as there are other types of gliders. The Rogallo is less expensive and easier to build. It will give you a basic building experience at a minimal cost and will be easier to fly once complete. Also, it can be built in less time than the more advanced designs and it can be re-sold at a higher price than you paid for materials.

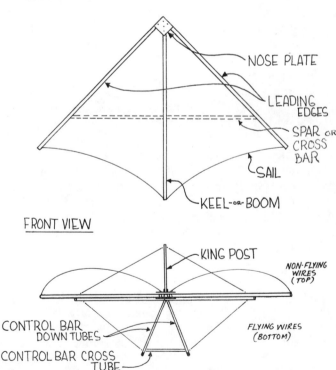

TOP VIEW

NOSE PLATE

LEADING EDGES

SPAR or CROSS BAR

SAIL

KEEL -or- BOOM

FRONT VIEW

KING POST

NON-FLYING WIRES (TOP)

CONTROL BAR DOWN TUBES

FLYING WIRES (BOTTOM)

CONTROL BAR CROSS TUBE

Anatomy of a Rogallo hang glider.

First, the backbone of every kite is the tubing. With weak tubing you have a weak kite and needless to say with strong tubing you have a strong kite. So, before you run out and lay down $150 for tubing, decide what you want in the way of strength and weight. For example: On a basic Rogallo, the wing tip is the weak point and this is the best place to set your minimum standards.

Know Your Aluminum

To start with, you have different alloys in aluminum, just as you have in steel. The main difference is that pure aluminum weighs about 172.8 pounds per cubic foot whereas pure iron weighs 483.84 pounds per cubic foot. When you figure that the average hang glider contains about 300 cubic inches or 30 pounds of aluminum, you realize that steel is out of the question for tubing unless you don't mind a Rogallo that weighs upwards of 94 pounds and must be painted once a week to stop rust.

With aluminum selected for a frame, I have some bad news and some good news. The bad news is that you have thousands of tubes to choose from with different alloys, wall thicknesses, tube diameters, and lengths. The good news is that it has all been worked out by engineers in the aircraft field and the two most commonly used alloys are 6061-T6 and 2024-T3. 6061-T6 has a tensile strength of 18,000 pounds maximum and is less expensive than 2024-T3. It is the most versatile of the heat treatable alloys, the most weldable, and the easiest to work with. It probably has the best availability of the alloys. 6061-T6 is solution heat treated, then artificially aged.

On the other hand, you have the impeccable 2024-T3 for those who want the pick of the crop and can afford it at almost five times the cost of 6061-T6. Its tensile strength is 70,000 pounds maximum, almost four times stronger than 6061-T6. 2024-T3 has excellent fatigue resistance, is easily machined but hard to weld, has poor corrosion resistance, and anodizing becomes a necessity. It is used mainly in aircraft products.

Next, you must decide what wall thickness to use. Tubing comes in the following wall thicknesses: .020, .022, .025, .028, .035, .042, .049, .050, .058, .065, .083, etc. Again, this has all been worked out and the most commonly used wall thicknesses are .049 and .058, with the exception of some control bars being built from .083. I have tried all of these and found that .058 is much stronger than .049. You will also find that .058 resists dents better and usually it is hard to find lengths longer than 12 feet. .058 wall is best if you need to sleeve because the next smaller tube diameter will slip fit nicely inside the 12-foot length with little or no movement.

Go for Strength

The other choice you must make is tube diameter. On this point I differ strongly from most of the manufacturers. Most Rogallos were constructed of 1½″ × .049 tubing when hang gliders first started out and the kites were about 16 or 17 feet long. As time went on, manufacturers found that a 16- or 17-foot kite would not lift many of the heavy pilots, so they increased the size of their kites but did not increase the diameter of their tubing or its wall thicknesses. They had a large stock of that size and in mild wind conditions it held up. But I feel the main reason is that it is lighter than larger diameter tubing.

For illustration purposes I will use 1½″ tubing and 2″ tubing on a hypothetical hang glider with cantilevered wing tips extending seven feet back from the cross bar. In this test we actually built and tested two frames to find the strength at the wing tips. These gliders were built to test tube diameters and wall tickness and do not represent any manufacturer's design. In the test we used 1½″ × .049 tubing of 6061-T6 alloy clamped to the cross bar with a sleeve holding it in place (as opposed to a hole for a bolt). We exerted a pressure of 91 pounds at the wing tip and the tube gave way. With another tube, we drilled a hole to bolt the leading edge to the cross bar and tried the same test. It failed at 52 pounds.

Then we tried a tube of 2″ × .058 wall and it failed at 172 pounds. This was a bending load which a hang glider succumbs to in a strong pullout or a strong gust.

The disadvantage of larger diameter tubing is weight. A kite with 80 feet of 1½″ × .049 tubing 6061-T6 will weigh 21 pounds and a kite with 80 feet of 2″ × .058 tubing 6061-T6 will weigh about 27 pounds, six pounds more; but it has more than three times the strength of the smaller diameter tubing. The choice is up to you, although I feel that high altitude flights demand the larger size. Since you don't carry the kite up the hill for the high flights (most are carried on trucks at big meets) the weight shouldn't matter.

Whatever your choice, try to use larger diameter tubes on the leading edges if at all possible. You can get by with 1½″ in the cross bar and keel because they are not normally subject to bending loads as the leading edges are.

Another idea is to use a leading edge king post, an extension of your cross bar by about one foot with cables running from the nose

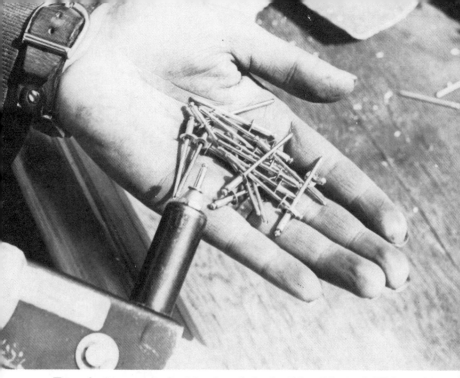

Top photo, a pop-rivet tool and rivets, ⅛" × ¼" steel. This tool will come with enough rivets to sleeve a complete glider and will cost under $7.00. Arrow in bottom photo shows a pop-rivet in place, holding sleeve into end of tube.

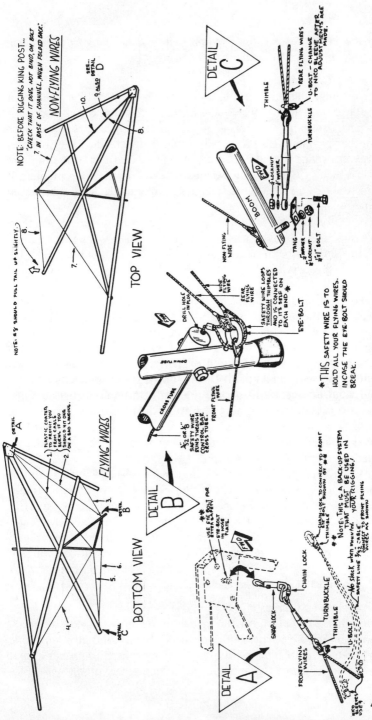

This and the following two illustration pages show details of a typical Rogallo-type hang glider, the Whitney Flying Wing.

47

to the tips of your cross bar and then to your wing tips. This will help keep your wing tips from bending.

Sleeved Construction

If you have picked out your tubing, let's say 2″ × .058, your next problem is length. Most gliders are 18 feet or longer and most tubing comes in 12-foot lengths. So, it appears that we have another problem. But, if we are using .058 wall, then we can use a sleeve to splice the tube together. Don't be alarmed at the thought of a splice in your tubing because, if done in the right manner, it will result in a tube that is stronger than a single length, unsleeved tube.

The Porta-Wing is made up of eleven tubes sleeved together. When a stress analysis was run on it, the Porta-Wing was stronger than a single tube unsleeved design. This is because it has a double thickness at the sleeve area. Instead of an .058 wall, you would have an .116 wall.

To make a longer tube out of two smaller tubes, anchor the sleeves by the use of pop-rivets of ⅛″ × ¼″ steel. You should use at least three around the diameter of the tube about 2″ from the seam where the two outside tubes fit together. The sleeve for a 2″ × .058 tube is 1⅞″ × .049 or .058 with a length of 18″ with nine inches extended into each end of the 2″ tube. If the sleeve is to be on a leading edge tube, it would be as far toward the nose as possible, because this is where you have less stress. The leading edge near the wing tip is subject to strong bending loads, a stress that is not beneficial to a sleeved tube. A compression load can be greatly dampened by the use of sleeves.

As an example, take a straw and place one end in the palm of each hand. Try to compress it until it breaks. You will notice that it bent before it finally collapsed. Now, take another straw and try the same thing with one exception. Have someone hold the center of the straw lightly to keep it from bending. This will represent a sleeve. Now try to compress it. You probably will, but you will also notice that it took more pressure to do so. Now you have an idea what a short sleeve in the right place can do.

Dowels and Bushings

Now that you have your tubing and know how to sleeve it, check the plans to see what length you need. Sleeve and cut the tubing as directed in the plans (most plans tell where to splice). Next, sleeve or reinforce the areas in the tubing where a bolt will be lo-

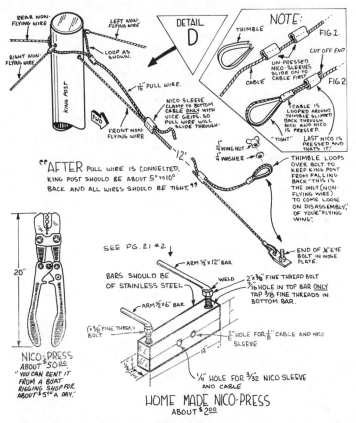

REAR NON-FLYING WIRE

LEFT NON-FLYING WIRE

RIGHT NON-FLYING WIRE

LOOP AS SHOWN.

KING POST

FWD

FRONT NON-FLYING WIRE

$\frac{1}{16}$" PULL WIRE.

NICO SLEEVE CLAMP TO BOTTOM CABLE ONLY WITH VICE GRIPS. SO PULL WIRE WILL SLIDE THROUGH.

DETAIL D

NOTE:

THIMBLE

FIG 1.

CUT OFF END

CABLE

UN-PRESSED NICO-SLEEVES SLIDE ON TO CABLE FIRST.

FIG 2

CABLE IS LOOPED AROUND THIMBLE SLIPPED BACK THROUGH NICO AND NICO IS PRESSED.

"TIGHT"

LAST NICO IS PRESSED AND THATS IT.

12'

$\frac{1}{4}$" WING NUT

$\frac{1}{4}$" WASHER

"AFTER PULL WIRE IS CONNECTED, KING POST SHOULD BE ABOUT 5° TO 10° BACK AND ALL WIRES SHOULD BE TIGHT."

THIMBLE LOOPS OVER BOLT TO KEEP KING POST FROM FALLING BACK. "THIS IS THE ONLY (NON-FLYING WIRE) TO COME LOOSE ON DISASSEMBLY, OF YOUR "FLYING WING".

END OF $\frac{1}{4}$" EYE BOLT IN NOSE PLATE.

20"

NICO-PRESS ABOUT $50.00
" YOU CAN RENT IT FROM A BOAT RIGGING SHOP FOR ABOUT $5.00 A DAY."

SEE PG. 21 #2

BARS SHOULD BE OF STAINLESS STEEL

ARM $\frac{1}{2}$" x 12" BAR

ARM $\frac{1}{2}$" x 6" BAR

$\frac{1}{4}$" $\frac{3}{8}$" FINE THREAD BOLT

WELD

2" x $\frac{3}{8}$" FINE THREAD BOLT
$\frac{7}{16}$" HOLE IN TOP BAR ONLY TAP $\frac{3}{8}$" FINE THREADS IN BOTTOM BAR.

$\frac{1}{8}$" HOLE FOR $\frac{1}{8}$" CABLE AND NICO SLEEVE

12"

$\frac{1}{2}$"

$\frac{1}{4}$" HOLE FOR $\frac{3}{32}$" NICO SLEEVE AND CABLE

HOME MADE NICO-PRESS
ABOUT $2.00

cated. This is to strengthen the area for the compression load resulting from the tightening of the bolts. This can be done by two sleeves like 1⅞" with a 1¼" inside it, slipped into the 2" tube. This will help hold a compression load. Some people use a wood dowel. If this method is used, paint the dowel with some type of waterproof finish to keep the wood from expanding because of moisture and splitting a tube. This may follow an unintended venture into a lake or ocean.

The next thing is drill the holes in your tubing and insert bushings in the holes. If specified in the plans this can be done with a special tool or with two flathead screws and a hammer.

First, cut a bushing from aluminum. Copper should not be used because it will start a galvanic reaction between the two dissimilar metals. Insert it into the hole drilled through the 2" tube. Let it extend ⅛″ out each end so that the bushing will be 2¼″ long. Insert a flathead screw into each end of the bushing. Lay the tube on a hard surface and hit the top screw with a hammer to start a flare. Then remove the screws and place a bolt with a washer on each end into the bushings and tighten the nut. This will flare it the rest of the way.

The ends of your tubing may be finished off with aluminum caps which can be obtained from any chain link fence company. Or you can buy rubber caps at some hardware stores that will work.

Readymade Hardware
Your next job is to find hardware such as nico sleeves, thimbles, cable, tangs, bolts, nuts or wing nuts, nose plate, swing seat, and turnbuckles. At the time I built my first glider, this meant about 150 miles of traveling. But thanks to the growth of the sport, many if not all, of the hardware items can be purchased by mail from companies manufacturing hang gliders, parts and hardware. Next is the construction or purchase of a swing seat or prone harness. In a later chapter I will discuss the main differences between the two to help you make a decision as to which is best for you.

To save time you can order a sail for your kite. Or, if you have an over-active thyroid, you can undertake the new career of sailmaker and proceed to put Betsy Ross to shame! If you just want to have it made by a professional, you should take your plans or a copy of them to the sailmaker. To save time, let him be making the sail while you build the rest of the kite. If the company you bought the plans from sells sails, it would be best to buy from them. They make the one type of sail, would know where the main stresses are, how to distribute the load, and how much billow to add.

All About Sails
For those of you who are going to make your own sail — and, for that matter, for those who aren't — remember: The sail makes the kite!

Regardless of the method of construction or design of the frame of your kite, it is only a skeleton until the sail is applied. This cover provides the airfoil and makes flying possible.

I am far from being a "clothes horse" but I have a big problem finding a readymade suit that fits me properly. After trying on several, I end up with a compromise fit, even after alterations.

Now, by the same token, if you want a sail that will allow your kite to perform as it should, you must have it tailored by a sail-

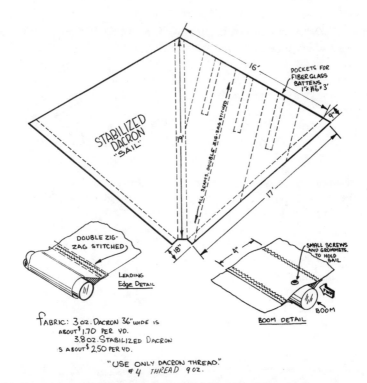

Typical layout and details for a Dacron hang glider sail.

maker who knows the aerodynamics involved in the design of the sail. Knowing how to use a sewing machine is a small part of sailmaking.

I have seen people with good performing kites switch from plastic to Dacron and the kite no longer flew properly. The sail is quite often the last thing suspected if made by a "reputable" sailmaker. This may come as a shock to some people but sailmakers are not infallible.

Sail Deficiencies

I would like to point to a few things to look at if your sail doesn't satisfy you.

Dacron is the most acceptable material for sails. Three-ounce to three-point-eight-ounce stabilized Dacron is used by most manufacturers.

Dacron is preferred because it is non-porous and has virtually no stretch to it. Materials that stretch tend to pocket around the seams.

51

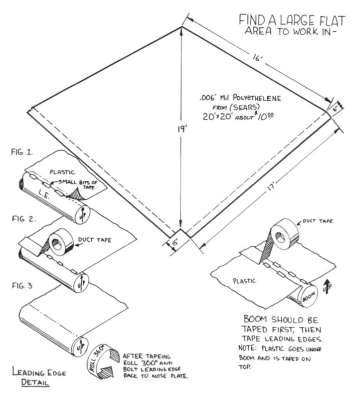

FIND A LARGE FLAT AREA TO WORK IN—

16'

.006" Mil Polyethelene FROM (SEARS) 20'x20' ABOUT $10.00

19'

6"

17'

15'

FIG 1.

PLASTIC

SMALL BITS OF TAPE.

L.E.

UP

FIG 2.

DUCT TAPE

UP

FIG. 3

DUCT TAPE

PLASTIC

UP

BOOM

UP

ROLL 360°

AFTER TAPEING ROLL 360° AND BOLT LEADING EDGE BACK TO NOSE PLATE.

LEADING EDGE DETAIL

BOOM SHOULD BE TAPED FIRST, THEN TAPE LEADING EDGES. NOTE: PLASTIC GOES UNDER BOOM AND IS TAPED ON TOP.

Plastic sheeting for hang glider sails is seldom used any more because of its vulnerability to snags. But for the low altitude, low budget do-it-yourselfer, it offers a possibility.

Seams should be lapped one-half-inch to five-eighths-of-an-inch and should have two rows of zig-zag stitching.

Pockets for tubes, particularly the leading edge tubes should be at least eight inches deep to perfect a smooth airfoil. Most pockets are much too small and cause considerable turbulence at a critical point on the sail.

Another thing to look for is hollow. Every sail should cut inward on an arc from the wing tip to the tail across the trailing edge. The amount varies with different kites and with different billow. Hollow is intended to prevent flapping. When this does not stop flapping at the trailing edge of the sail, battens are often added. In my judgment, adding battens is only "compounding a felony." We should be looking for the root cause of the flapping. Two common causes are in the design or the structure of the kite.

As for design, the kite with a very low aspect ratio is a more likely candidate for flapping. Sometimes the trailing edge is not giving lift, just creating drag. Nothing a pair of scissors couldn't cure.

Structure Affects Sail

As for structure, undersize tubing can be a contributing factor. Undersize leading edge tubes bend inward and upward in flight and put slack in the trailing edge of the sail causing flapping.

This condition is a two-way street. Undersize tubing can bend and contribute to flapping. And flapping can bend leading edge tubes.

If your leading edge tube breaks in flight due to fatigue from this constant flapping, it might give you something to think about as you are falling. Did my predicament originate from an incorrectly made sail or undersized tubing?

On the other hand, if you will give a little thought to the cause of flapping and get to the root of the trouble, you may be around to read hang gliding magazines.

When you see a sail with no battens flying and performing with little or no flapping, you can consider the kite and the sail to be designed correctly.

Billow is an important factor in the performance of any sail. Increasing billow will create more drag, decrease speed, give poor glide, increase stability, increase the angle of attack.

Rigging

Last but not least is your rigging. This is the part of building a hang glider that seems to throw most people. But thanks to the increasing interest in the sport, you can purchase cable pre-rigged for the brand of hang glider you are building. Most of these cable kits are available from the manufacturers and this may be the way you want to go. It is the best way if you have no rigging experience. If you are a do-it-yourselfer, there are some things to watch for when rigging. The first step is to purchase the parts and tools needed. This array of equipment consists of about 150 feet of 3/32″ diameter or ⅛″ diameter stainless or galvanized carbon steel cable. 7 × 7 is commonly used because of its high abrasion resistance. It is more flexible than 1 × 7 or 1 × 9. 7 × 7 simply means that you have 7 bundles of 7 wires twisted into a single bundle. The breaking strength of 3/32″ 7 × 7 galvanized is 920 pounds, the same as

Top photo, Roman numerals denote the 7 strands in a 7 × 7 cable, and Arabic numerals show the 7 independent wires that compose each strand. Bottom photo shows a typical cable end with tang: A) stainless tang 1″ × 2″ × ⅛″ thick; B) 3/32 stainless thimble slipping off the other side of the cable because cable was not pulled tight before swedging the first nico sleeve; (C); (D) second nico sleeve used mainly to cover end of the excess cable.

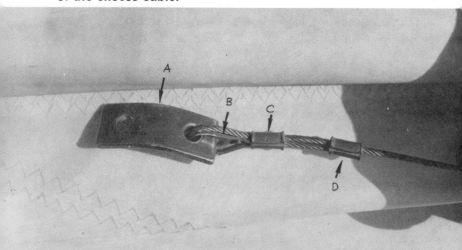

3/32″ 7 × 7 stainless. The breaking strength of ⅛″ 7 × 7 is 2,000 pounds galvanized and only 1,760 pounds for stainless. As you can see, galvanized cable is not weaker than stainless but sometimes stronger and it is about 1/3 the cost.

As mentioned before, tubing is the weak link of a kite and not cable. Out of the many hundreds of accidents I have seen (in which very few people got hurt) I have only seen one cable snap and that was on a home-built kite utilizing 1/16″ cable with ⅛″ nico sleeves, gracefully wedged with a 25-pound sledge hammer.

One more point about cable is that you should not leave the end protruding out of the last nico sleeve or it will fray and cause snags in your sail. Fray is the main reason for two nico sleeves, not strength as many think.

Tools for rigging will sometimes cost more than the cable. Unless you are planning on going into the rigging business, they can be borrowed or rented from a nearby boat yard by the following names: swaging tool, about $50.00 if purchased; and Felco cable cutters, about $10.00.

The seated position is much more comfortable than prone but creates more drag.

7. Swing Seat vs. Prone Harness

Many people ask which is the best way to fly, swing seat or prone harness? After flying both, I have found that if you are going to become a serious pilot, you should start out in the swing seat. If you are only going to fly small hills and comfort is not important, then prone is more thrilling.

Everything has its good points and its bad points and the swing seat and the prone harness are no exceptions. For example, the cost of a good swing seat is anywhere from $20.00 to $30.00 compared to $60.00 to $80.00 for a good prone harness. A swing seat is easy to put on and to take off while some prone harnesses take up to five minutes to put on. As for comfort, a 10-minute flight in a prone harness is about all a person can take because your legs get tired, your neck gets cramps and the straps start to dig into your shoulders. A swing seat can be as comfortable as a chair and people have flown a kite being towed behind a boat for over 15 hours, something that could never be done in a prone harness. Another point is that nobody has ever set an endurance record in a prone harness, only in swing seats.

The main point is that in a swing seat your weight or center of gravity (C.G.) is lower, about 50% lower, so you don't have to move as far to control, and with a lower C.G. your hang glider is more stable.

Some believe that the prone position gives extra pitch control by getting you all the way over the control bar. But if your glider is rigged properly, you should never need it. In a swing seat, you can pull the bar only to your chest. Others claim that the prone position reduces drag and is more aerodynamically sound and streamlined.

A disadvantage I have found with a swing seat is that it is a little harder to launch with than a prone harness. In a prone harness you just slowly fall into a prone position while running. In a swing seat you have a reciprocating motion involved in your launch. First, you run forward, then you leap back into the seat, which is not all that natural to the newcomer. This often results in a new pilot flying prone in a swing seat the first few times. If the swing seat is not tight or the flyer is not using a crotch strap, he will wind up with the seat around his chest, which will blow all his chances for "the most graceful pilot of the year award."

One Swing Seat Hazard
The biggest danger I have found with the swing seat is that a new pilot will sometimes get into a dive situation and thinking he may not pull out, puts his feet forward to protect himself in case of a bad landing. Without knowing it, he has forced himself into a steeper dive that was caused by the extra weight of the pilot's legs.

If you think that your legs won't make that much difference, next time you fly a kite use only your legs for pitch control. You will be amazed at the amount of control you get from a little movement of your legs. This is caused by the moment of the weight being far from the kite. You don't need much weight shift to change pitch angle and once you realize this, cross your legs and fly with them tucked under you.

If you decide to fly swing seat, be sure that the seat is sturdy. Most of those used are children's play equipment swing seats. It is also important that the connecting lines be made of plastic coated cable and not rope. Many times I have seen rope give way and people get hurt. The rope apparently becomes old and worn, then breaks. On the other hand, cable is obviously stronger, lasts longer, and will give you warning long before it breaks.

Make sure this cable goes under the seat in case your seat gives way. The cables will support you until you land. Just have the connecting lines continue down under the seat then back up the other side. The cable should be plastic coated to protect your body from abrasions or cable burns. Your seat should be positioned so the horizontal control bar comes to your elbow height. Any higher or lower can be uncomfortable and dangerous. When rigging or putting together your connecting lines, measure them to be sure of the proper and necessary length.

This is Dave Muehl of Eipper Formance demonstrating the prone position. He firmly believes it to be the best all around flying position. Photo by Downie and Associates.

SWING SEAT

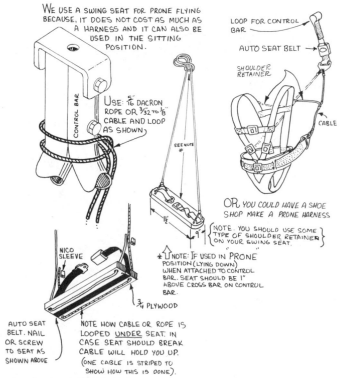

We use a swing seat for prone flying because, it does not cost as much as a harness and it can also be used in the sitting position.

CONTROL BAR

Use: 5/16 DACRON ROPE OR 3/32 to 8/... CABLE AND LOOP AS SHOWN)

LOOP FOR CONTROL BAR

AUTO SEAT BELT →

SHOULDER RETAINER

CABLE

SEE NOTE *

1½"

9"

OR you could have a shoe shop make a prone harness

NOTE. You should use some type of shoulder retainer on your swing seat.

*↑NOTE: If used in PRONE POSITION (LYING DOWN) WHEN ATTACHED TO CONTROL BAR. SEAT SHOULD BE 1" ABOVE CROSS BAR ON CONTROL BAR.

NICO SLEEVE

3/4 PLYWOOD

AUTO SEAT BELT. NAIL OR SCREW TO SEAT AS SHOWN ABOVE

NOTE HOW CABLE OR ROPE IS LOOPED UNDER SEAT. IN CASE SEAT SHOULD BREAK CABLE WILL HOLD YOU UP. (ONE CABLE IS STRIPED TO SHOW HOW THIS IS DONE).

A page from the Whitney Enterprises plan set showing basic swing seat construction.

Crotch Strap and Cable Position

But most important, have a crotch strap in the center of your seat. This is to prevent the seat from slipping up on you during flight. It consists of two-inch webbing pulled through the front center of the seat. When you get ready to buckle in to fly, the continuous loop crotch strap will come from the seat between your legs up to your lap where the seat belt will slip through it to buckle. When the seat belt is released, it should slip out of the crotch strap without snagging for quick release. The seat belt should also be made of two-inch webbing, running under the seat for safety reasons, then pop-riveted onto the sides of the seat, with a buckle at one end.

When flying seated, you must make the decision to fly with the cables in front or in back. If the cables (connecting lines) are behind your back, you are not as likely to fall back on take-off. But most important, in a bad landing (which all of us have once in a while) you won't pivot up through the control bar and hit your head on the boom or keel, as you would if the cables were in front of you. Some say if the cables are behind you, you tend to fall forward on take-off, but I have found it very unlikely because you are holding onto the control bar which supports you.

Good Prone Harness

If you do decide to fly prone, the first thing is to get a good harness, one that will fit right and, most important, one that is comfortable. The harnesses on the market now tend to dig into your shoulders, making it very uncomfortable when flying for prolonged periods of time.

When buying or making a harness, make sure it has a three-point suspension at the shoulder, the hips, and the thighs made of webbing two-inches wide and 1/16-inches thick. This will assure you the strength and sturdiness you need. You want the assurance that the prone harness will hold up when you are up there.

There should be a quick-release between the pilot and the harness for emergencies. When landing in water or in gusty winds, the kite wants to flip over and you want to get out fast. When flying seated this isn't necessary because you have a quick release buckle with the seat.

Some pilots have told me that flying prone is safer than flying seated because on a crash landing you slide on the ground on your stomach and that's a lot better than skimming the ground on your tail bone. But they don't mention the sudden stop after the slide. You tend to pivot up through the control bar and, more than likely, hit your head on the boom or keel tube. Always wear a helmet when flying either prone or seated.

To confuse the issue even further, there is another choice for those who can't make up their minds. It's a new invention called the prone swing seat harness that is being worked on by a few companies. It simply lets you try both positions on the same flight, and it works out great. You can take off in the prone position and, when you get to your desired altitude, flop over into the seated position for comfort. Later, when landing, you can land either prone or seated and be one step ahead of everyone else.

Tow kites are spectacular water show attractions. They can be towed to remarkable heights, cut loose, and make controlled landings. Their structures and flying techniques can be quite different from foot-launched kites.

8. Tow Kites

In the early 1960's at Cypress Gardens, Florida, a strange new sport was created when a small group of water skiers found a way to get airborne while being towed behind a boat by the use of a five-sided, flat kite. However, it was soon realized that the new kite had very pronounced limitations, such as stability and control. As skiers plummeted in left and right, a newer kite appeared, introduced in the late '60's by Bill Bennett, which became an instant success. The kites could now be released and allowed to come to a controlled landing.

Since then ski kites have been used all over the world with much success. The only real danger is of a tow rope breaking; an accidental release while under tow which would result in an outside loop; and a structural failure due to the absence of what is now known as a king post. With these limitations understood, the pilots of ski kites have better safety records than the pilots launching from land. The sports are quite similar. A "land" pilot may use a truck to carry his kite to the top of a hill while the "sea" pilot will be towed by a boat as a means of getting to "the top of the hill." After take-off, both pilots function much the same. The main reason for towing at Cypress Gardens is that there are few hills in Florida and so it's either tow or don't fly.

Bill Bennett, the greatest exponent of tow kites, is noted for some astonishing flying exploits.

Facing page, hang gliding made its Hollywood debut in style when Roger Moore (James Bond 007) flew a Delta Wing Kite in "Live and Let Die." Center, a covey of the smaller tow kites used in the water show at Cypress Gardens, Fla. and bottom, in October, 1973, Rudy Kishazy literally topped everybody. He flew from the summit of Mt. Blanc in the French Alps (altitude, 15,766 feet) to the valley of Servoz below (altitude, 2,624 feet) using a modified hang glider.

Differences

The tow kite differs little from the glider used in foot launching as far as appearance. But structurally it differs greatly. To begin with, it is normally of a smaller size, allowing greater flying speed and less drag while towing. It has no top flying wires or king post due to the fact that it is seldom parked on its nose in a strong wind.

The control bar of a tow kite is built from stainless steel instead of aluminum. It has an "A" frame attached to the cross tube with a tow rope release located at the apex of the structure. This is for the strength needed for towing.

Other differences include $\frac{1}{8}$-inch bottom wires and a set of floats, one being located at the tail of the kite and one on each side of the control bar.

Tow kites are an advanced type flying machine which should not be attempted without first consulting an expert on the type of tow kite you are going to fly.

The sport of skysurfing consists mainly of foot-launched kites and so much more information on tow kites is inappropriate. First learn to foot launch and then learn to tow from an expert, not a book. Some believe ski kiting should be classified as another sport, just as the different types of car races are differentiated. There are publications on the sport which are very informative and list dealers of ski kites. It can be acquired by sending to Cypress Gardens for information.

9. Motor-powered Kites

To many people, the addition of a power source to a hang glider is nothing less than a mortal sin because of the noise and pollution. But the people who complain the most are the same ones who will use a four-wheel drive, gas-guzzling, eight-cylinder tank to carry their kite to the top of the 25-foot hill they're flying.

There is nothing wrong about being a purist, but if you are against motors on kites then you should practice what you preach and use a non-polluting device to transport your kite. If you're not quite that devoted, then you might as well step back and make room for the kite of the future which will sport twin pressure jets, have a range of about 50 miles, and a top speed of about the same.

During World War II, there were predictions that after the war there would be a small plane in every garage. But after the war, the planes seemed to get bigger and more powerful, so the chance for many to fly was postponed. Then came the new sport of sky-surfing and with it came the possibility that someone would remember unfulfilled hopes of World War II.

If used and not abused, a motor can add to the sport! It can give hope to the thousands of people who live in flat areas with no wind. It could also be used as a safety device in case a pilot gets into a sink area, needs extra power to clear a certain hazard, or maybe just to get enough altitude to do some real soaring. Whatever the reason, power packs should not be condemned without a good trial.

Many Attempts
There have been many attempts to add power to hang gliders. One of the first was by N.A.S.A., which invented the Rogallo wing. Another was by Ryan Aircraft and another by Bill Bennett of Delta Wing Kite Company. Bennett had a new approach to the old problem. Where to put a motor on a hang glider?

What appears to be a throwback to Flash Gordon is a U.S. Navy "Aercab," an Escape/Rescue System under testing. It uses weight shift just as hang gliders do. Photo by Don Dwiggins.

After many suggestions from competitors, Bennett decided it would be more comfortable on his back, which is where he puts it whenever he wants to show someone how to get to the top of a hill the easy way. Bill's mutation at one time used a go-kart racing engine manufactured by McCulloch. It now sports a three-bladed propeller and has a tuned exhaust. He has added a quick-release to the back-pack and caged the prop in a wire shield for safety.

I have seen him fly at meets with complete control and I have heard the high pitched sound of his back-pack as he flew off into the sunset. Bill Bennett has had many years of practice with his back-pack and he is probably the best authority on the subject of motors for kites. If more information is required, you can contact him at Delta Wing Kite Co., P.O. Box 438, Van Nuys, California 91408.

Many other motors have been tried. Some with success, some without success. I have spent hours talking with Joe Faust of Low and Slow magazine about ecology-type power, storage systems for kites. One idea discussed is air-powered motors which could work off a scuba tank. One of the advantages of an air-powered motor is instant power (as quick as you could turn a valve). As much as 3,000 pounds of air pressure is now being contained in the new aluminum tanks. There's no noise, no pollution, and above all, low cost.

Other ideas are rubber-band type storage systems to power a

The Porta-Jet is another attempt at powered hang gliding. Using throttle-controlled jets, it is a joint venture of Whitney Enterprises and EMG Engineering.

Ryan Aeronautical has produced a flock of designs in the flex-wing family. This Fleep is a motor-powered cargo carrier capable of lifting close to 1,000 pounds. Photo by Ryan.

prop mounted on the tail. It could be wound by a bicycle pedal set-up or could be a system using the wind to wind up the rubber band.

Electric motors could be used to get you up, leaving the batteries on the ground and using a 200-foot cord plugged into your control bar. When at 200 feet, the line would unplug and drop to earth to be used for the next launch.

Another possibility is a jet engine which is offered by EMG Engineering, at 18518 South Broadway, Gardena, California 90248. I checked into the jets and they have a lot of possibilities for a power source. The main advantages are weight (11 pounds), power (40 pounds of thrust) and the fact that they have few moving parts. They will someday be tested on a kite and more facts will be available on them as power sources for kites.

Power Inevitable

As you can see, there is no way of stopping motors from entering the sport, so the best thing is to make sure that power is not abused or used ignorantly. As to the purity of the sport being blemished, I see no difference in towing a kite up into the air with a 200 h.p. boat or using an 18 h.p. back pack to achieve altitude. They both use power, they both pollute, and they both make noise. If you are still down on motors, fine! But you should start by carrying your kite to the flying site, or at least carry your kite up the hill. I have never gone up a hill in a truck because I believe that if you can't carry your kite to the top, it's too high. Also, sometimes going up the hill carrying a kite is as much of a challenge as flying down and it has a tendency to separate the men from the boys.

Motor powered hang gliders may be the answer to many of to-day's problems. For the Coast Guard patroling the shore, a motor-powered kite with pontoons could be supplied at a fraction of the cost of a helicopter. It would be easy to store, carry heavy loads, and it would be better for training because of the ease of operation. The police and hospitals could some day be using them. I have seen films of a Rogallo taking off and doing figure eights in the width of a runway, about 10 feet off the ground. Then it made a perfect landing in what appeared to be about 15 feet. You have to admit that is pretty impressive. Who knows, maybe someday you may walk out to your garage and take out a three-wheeled chassis, at-tach your hang glider to the top bar, take off down the street, fly to your local skysurfing hill, land, detach your kite, and spend the rest of the day skysurfing.

10. Manufacturers, Clubs, Publications

ARIZONA
Manufacturers
Hang Gliders, Inc.
1300 East Valencia
Tucson, Az. 85706

Rainco
P.O. Box 20944
Phoenix, Az. 85036

ARKANSAS
Manufacturer
Stanley Newton
P.O. Box 163 Rt. 5
Hot Springs, Ak. 71901

CALIFORNIA
Clubs and Organizations
Delta Birdman
1047 N. Wilcox Ave.
Los Angeles, Ca. 90083

Kydid Flyer Club
323 Euclid #140
Santa Ana, Ca. 92703

Orange County Sky Sailing
  Club
916 Delaware
Huntington Beach, Ca. 92648

Self Soar Assn.
Box 1869
Santa Monica, Ca. 90406

The Fellow Feathers
2123 Junipero Serra Blvd.
Daly City, Ca. 94015

CALIFORNIA (cont.)

Ultralight Flyers Organization
P.O. Box 81665
San Diego, Ca. 92138

U.S. Hang Gliding Assn.
P.O. Box 66306
Los Angeles, Ca. 90066

Wings of Rogallo
1137 Jamestown Dr.
Sunnyvale, Ca. 94087

Manufacturers
Delta Wing Kites
P.O. Box 483
Van Nuys, Ca. 91408

Dyna Soar, Inc.
3581 Cahuenga Blvd.
Hollywood, Ca. 90068

Eipper Formance Inc.
P.O. Box 246
Lomita, Ca. 90717

Free Flight Systems
12424 Gladstone Av.
Sylmar, Ca. 81342

Jack Hall
12561 Pearce St.
Garden Grove, Ca. 92643

Northern Calif. Sun
P.O. Box 1624
Sausalito, Ca. 94965

Pacific Gull
1321 Calle Valle
San Clemente, Ca. 92672

Seagull Aircraft
1554 5th Av.
Santa Monica, Ca. 90401

Sport Kites, Inc.
1202 E. Walnut
Santa Ana, Ca. 92701

Taras Kiceniuk, Jr.
Palomar Observatory
Palomar Mountain, Ca. 92060

The Bike and Sport Shoppe
P.O. Box 404
Bishop, Ca. 93514

The Bird People
Box 43
Sun Valley, Ca. 91352

True Flight
1719 Hillsdale Av.
San Jose, Ca. 95124

Ultralite Products
137 Oregon St.
El Segundo, Ca. 90245

Ultralight Suppliers
4632 Palm Dr.
La Canada, Ca. 91011

Volmar Aircraft
Box 5222
Glendale, Ca. 91201

Whitney Enterprises
P.O. Box 90762s
Los Angeles, Ca. 90009

Magazines
Delta Kite Flyer News
P.O. Box 483
Van Nuys, Ca. 91408

Kiting News Letter
2243 San Anseline Av.
Long Beach, Ca. 90815

Man-Flite Magazine
P.O. Box 90762s
Los Angeles, Ca. 90009

Gary Warren
502 Barkentine Lane
Redwood City, Ca. 90465

COLORADO
Clubs and Organizations
North American Sky Sailing
 Assn.
350 Colorado Blvd.
Denver, Co. 80206
Manufacturers
Chandelle Sky Sails
15955 5th Ave.
Golden, Co. 80401

Jeff Campbell
Box 103
Telluride, Co. 81435

CONNECTICUT
Manufacturers
Sky Sports, Inc.
Ellington Airport
Ellington, Ct. 06029

Zephyr Aircraft Corp.
25 Mill St.
Glastonbury, Ct. 06033

One of the hang glider manufacturers who didn't make it was a Frenchman named Besnier in 1678.

DISTRICT OF COLUMBIA
Manufacturer
East Coast Hang Gliders Ltd.
P.O. Box 961
Washington, D.C. 20044

FLORIDA
Clubs and Organizations
Ascension Island Hang
Glider Ass.
NASA/SDTN STN Ascension Island
P.O. Box A
Patrick AFB, Fl. 32975
Manufacturers
Don R. Hill
P.O. Box 2868
Sarasota, Fl. 33578

Hollymatic Corp.

FLORIDA (cont.)
2001 N W 51st St.
Boca Raton, Fl. 33432

GEORGIA
Clubs and Organizations
Atlanta Ultralight Assn.
190 Shiloh Rd.
Kenesaw, Ga. 30144

HAWAII
Clubs and Organizations
Pacific Tradewind Sky-Sailors
3142 Hinano St.
Honolulu, Hawaii 96815

IDAHO
Clubs and Organizations
Mountain Home Glider Riders
Box 3414
Mountain Home AFB, Id.
83648

INDIANA
Manufacturers
Dyna Soar Mfg. Co.
P.O. Box 236
Carmel, In. 46032

Hoosier Hang Gliders
707 Highwood
Greencastle, In. 46185

MAINE
Manufacturer
Sky Truckin', Inc.
P.O. Box 234
Biddeford, Me. 04005

MARYLAND
Manufacturers
Greg Molenaar
5603 McKinley St.
Bethesda, Md. 20034

Sport Flight
3305 Ferndale St.
Kensington, Md. 20795

MASSACHUSETTS
Clubs and Organizations
New England Hang Gliding
Assn.
P.O. Box 356
Stoughtn, Ma. 02072

Windward Gliding Club
901 Plum St.
Ft. Davons, Ma. 01433
Manufacturers
Man-Flight Systems, Inc.
P.O. Box 375
Marlboro, Ma. 01752

Dana L. Littlefield
97 Piney Point Dr.
Centerville, Ma. 02632

MASSACHUSETTS (cont.)
Niemi Manufacturing Co.,
Inc.
25 Willow St.
Fitchburg, Ma. 01420

Manta East
1 Veteran Rd.
Woburn, Ma. 01801

Sky Sports
P.O. Box 441
Whitman, Ma. 02382
Magazines
Skysurfer Mag.
P.O. Box 872
Worcester, Ma. 01613

MICHIGAN
Clubs and Organizations
Michigan U.F.O. Hang
Glider Club
c/o Connie Malouin
1554 Park Lane
Livonia, Mi. 48154

Michigan Skysurfers
1361 Oregon
Pontiac, Mi. 48054
Manufacturers
AA Flight Systems
102 W Buffalo
New Buffalo, Mi. 48116

Jim Davis
987 Femmwood Circle
North Muskegon, Mi. 49445

Delta Wing of Mich.
1434 Lake Dr. SE
Grand Rapids, Mi. 49506

Thomas Drewek
27-73 Bonnie Dr.
Warren, Mi. 48093

MICHIGAN (cont.)

Gar's Sport Center
2531 So. Division Center
Grand Rapids, Mi. 49507

Felix Marine
14023 Green
Grand Haven, Mi. 49417

Said Boat Center
22 44th St. SE
Grand Rapids, Mi. 49509

MINNESOTA
Clubs and Organizations

Northwestern Hang Gliders
Assn.
212 15th Ave.
Minneapolis, Mn. 55404

Aircraft Unlimited
P.O. Box 1616
Minneapolis, Mn. 55111

MONTANA
Clubs and Organizations

Inland Empire
c/o Bill Johnson
P.O. Box 2009
Missoula, Mt. 59801

Manufacturer

Upward Bound
Box 2009
Missoula, Mt. 59801

NEW JERSEY
Clubs and Organizations

New Jersey Water Ski Kite
Assn.
40 Center
Springfield, N.J. 07081

Manufacturer

Vernon Valley Recreation
Rt. 94
Vernon, N.J. 07462

NEW MEXICO
Manufacturers

Kittyhawk Hang Gliders
3202 San Mateo
Albuquerque, N.M. 87110

NEW YORK
Manufacturers

Chandelle Birch Hill Inc.
P.O. Box 283
Patterson, N.Y. 12563

Cole Hill Recreational, Inc.
c/o Charles Miller
Box 193
Berne, N.Y. 12023

David Deming
Hoag Lane
Fayetteville, N.Y. 13066

David Inglehart
160 Ten Eyck St.
Watertown, N.Y. 13601

Long Island Kite Distrib.
5 Bethpage Rd.
Hicksville, N.Y. 11801

McCarron Aeronautical Corp.
17 Vichy Dr.
Saratoga Springs, N.Y. 12866

New York Hang Glider, Inc.
144-45 35th Ave.
Flushing, N.Y. 11354

NORTH CAROLINA
Clubs and Organizations

North Carolina Hang Gliding
Society
104 Wright St.
Lewisville, N.C. 27023

Manufacturers

Emory Gliders

Poor practice. After bending a wing tip in a bad landing, they proceed to bend it straight again. This is the main cause for wing tip failure. If a wing tip bends, replace it.

NORTH CAROLINA (cont.)
409 S. Dawson
Raleigh, N.C. 27601

Land, Sea and Air Ventures
P.O. Box 275
Wrightsville Beach, N.C.
28480

OHIO
Clubs and Organizations
Ohio Hang Glider Assn.
26875 Bagley
Olmstead Falls, Oh. 44138

OREGON
Clubs and Organizations
Oregon Hang Gliding Assn.
P.O. Box 3815

OREGON (cont.)
Portland, Or. 97208
Manufacturers
Rex Miller
643 East 8th Av.
Eugene, Or. 97401

PENNSYLVANIA
Clubs and Organizations
Eastern Penn. Hang Glider
Assn.
620 Walnut St.
Reading, Pa. 19601
Manufacturers
Icarus Inc.
228 So. Allen St.
State College, Pa. 16801

Icarus, Inc.

P.O. Box 51
Broomall, Pa. 19008

J.R. McTammany, MD.
620 Walnut St.
Reading, Pa. 19601

Sutton Bros.
222 Verbeke St.
Marysville, Pa. 17093

TENNESSEE
Manufacturer
Butterfly Ind. Inc.
1911 W. Cumberland Ave.
Knoxville, Tn. 37916

TEXAS
Clubs and Organizations
North Texas Hang Glider
Society
1716 Jasmine Lane
Plano, Tx. 75014
Manufacturers
Jim Foreman
4335 Mesa Circle
Amarillo, Tx. 79109

So. Central Kite and Glider
Enterprises
5206 Greenville Ave.
Dallas, Tx. 75014

UTAH
Clubs and Organizations
Utah Ultralight Gliders Assn.
143 East 500 N.
Kaysville, Ut. 84037

VIRGINIA
Clubs and Organizations
Capitol Hang Glider Assn.
7358 Shenandoah Ave.
Annandale, Va. 22003

Tidewater Hang Glider Club
c/o Otto F. Horton Jr.
5624 Hampshire Lane #102
Virginia Beach, Va. 23462
Manufacturer
John Luck
4610 Killam Ave.
Norfolk, Va. 23508

WASHINGTON
Clubs and Organizations
Eastern Washington Hang
Glider Assn.
1425 Marshall
Richland, Wa. 99352

Pacific Northwest Hang
Glider Assn.
417 Harvard Ave. #4
Seattle, Wa. 98102
Manufacturers
Skysails, Inc.
1110 East Pike
Seattle, Wa. 98123

The Flying Burriot Bros.
17036 44th NE
Seattle, Wa. 98155

WISCONSIN
Clubs and Organizations
Madison Sky Sailors
c/o Mark Langenfield
2861 Guilford Rd. #5
Madison, Wi. 53713
Manufacturers
Bonn Industries
434 West Rawson Ave.
Oak Creek, Wi. 53154

Fish Creek's Cycles
Rt. Exploration Outfitter
Fish Creek, Wi. 54212

WISCONSIN (cont.)
Aspen Enterprises
Box 425
Neenah, Wi. 54956

AUSTRALIA
Clubs and Organizations
T.A.S.S.A.
45 Lansdowne Parade
Oatley N.S.W. 2223
Australia
Manufacturer
Southern Cross
Box 21
Doveton, Victoria
Australia

CANADA
Clubs and Organizations
Alberta Hang Glider Assn.
131 10th Ave. S.E.
Calgary, Alberta
Canada

Southern Ontario Hang
Glider Assn.
10 Governors Rd.
Dundas, Ontario L9H 3J6
Canada

Westcoast Skysurfers Hang
Gliding Club
4660 W Tenth Ave. #1205
Vancouver, B.C. V6R 2J6
Canada
Manufacturers
Mini Sport
10 Governors Rd.
Dundas, Ontario
Canada

High Perspective RR #2
RR#2 Claremont
Ontario LOH 1EO

CANADA (cont.)
Canada

Muller Kites Ltd.
Box 4062 Postal Station C/P
Calgary, Alberta T2T 5M9
Canada

Tod Mountain Flying School
749 Victoria
Kamloops, B.C.
Canada

Kitsilano Marine and
Lumber Ltd.
1502 West 2nd Av.
Vancouver, B.C.
Canada

ENGLAND
Clubs and Organizations
National Hang Gliding Assn.
9 the Drive
West Wickham, Kent BR4
OEF
England

Sussex Para Kite Club
20 Surrenden
Brighten 6, Sussex
BNI 6PP England

British Kite Soaring Ass.
c/o Dick Bickel
8A Richman Close
Woodley, Berkshire
England
Manufacturers
McBroom Sailwings Ltd.
12 Manor Court Dr.
Horfield Dommon, Bristol
England BS7 OXF

L. Gabriels
4 Thornlea Av.

Hollinwood, Oldham,
Lancs, England

Alec M. Hunt
130 Houslow Rd.
Whitton, Twickenham,
Middlesex England

NEW ZEALAND
Clubs and Organizations
New Zealand Hang Gliding
Assn.
62 Nile Rd.
Westlake, Auckland 10,

New Zealand

SOUTH AFRICA
Manufacturers
South African Aviation Centre
P.O. Box 33191
Jeppestown, Transvall,
South Africa

SWITZERLAND
Manufacturer
Para Centro Locarno
Aeroporto Cantonale
6596 Gordola, Locarno
Switzerland

11. Who's Who in Hang Gliding

I have heard many theories to explain the growth of the sport of skysurfing. Some think the growth is caused by the ecology movement while others believe it was brought on by man's eternal quest for flight. But I believe differently. I feel all these things are contributing factors but the catalyst which inspires the sport are the people. They are not just everyday, common, garden variety of people but people with the widest range of personalities ever assembled in one place at one time.

Many of the personalities blend together in perfect harmony, some clash in bitter disputes, but all of them work together for the betterment of the sport. I don't think you can find one person in the sport of skysurfing who can be classified as an average person. Maybe it's because this sport is not your average sport, but a sport for people who think for themselves and are not afraid to be classified as "some kind of a nut" by the "average individual." So, a book about the sport of skysurfing is not complete without some mention of the people who made it all happen.

I have not met everyone involved in the sport of skysurfing, but the few I have met have impressed me, some favorably, some not so favorably, but nonetheless I will try to mention them as fairly as possible. After all, being a manufacturer, I tend to differ with other manufacturers on certain points. But I feel, or at least hope, we have come to accord on one point, and that is safety and its promotion above all else, including the sport itself.

Bill Bennett

First, a competitor, a pilot, and a friend. His name is Bill Bennett. I first met Bill at a meet held in San Francisco at a park called Coyote Hills. When you first meet Bill you either like him or you dislike him. It's that simple, there is no in between. He is the type of person who says what he believes and says it with no holds barred. He is very honest and people not ready for honesty are offended. But even people who dislike him have a great deal of respect for

Francis Rogallo, designer of the flexible wing kite now used in skysurfing. He originated his design 26 years ago while an engineer at Langley Research Center but, as a sport, little happened with skysurfing until 1969. Photo by Downie and Associates.

him. Bill is not the type of person who demands respect. He is the kind of person who has earned respect. As a pilot of a hang glider, he has clocked more hours in the air than most pilots of airplanes. In 1972, Bill leaped from Dante's View in Death Valley for a flight lasting 11 minutes, 47 seconds and covering 6.2 miles from an altitude of 5,757 feet. It was featured on The Thrillseekers television program.

Bill has probably set more world records than any other pilot

Bob Wills, at left, is the most extraordinary flyer skysurfing has yet produced. He has repeatedly set endurance records and has stayed aloft in a hang glider for more than eight hours at the time of this publication. Here he talks with Charles Schuck of the F.A.A. Photo by Downie and Associates.

alive today. At one event, he managed to be the first pilot to put a Delta-Wing through a loop with an altitude loss of some 800 feet. Of course, it was an accident which occurred when a tow rope snapped. But it didn't slow him down or scare him off. He continued to fly and set records until the boom in skysurfing reached the point where Bill had to put aside his first love and concentrate on business. Now Bill is either answering telephone calls or filling orders at Delta Wing Kites. And someday when the sport levels off, you will once again see Bill Bennett leaping off a distant hill with one of his gliders.

Bob Wills

While in San Francisco I met Bob Wills who used to fly for Bill Bennett until he decided to become enterprising and started his own company which he calls Sport Kites. Bob Wills is not only a good pilot but quite a showman, too. As a matter of fact, the first time I saw Bob he was upside down with his kite, a position which Bob found quite normal, or so it appears. He seemed to spend most of his time that way. That is, when he is not flying backwards. Most people think that Bob Wills is a show-off, but he does not impress me as one. He appears to be a person to whom flying comes naturally. Bob is a pilot who can turn a disastrous take-off into part of his stunt flying routine. He is not trying to impress anyone, as you find out when you meet him. Others want to imitate him and, because of his concern with safety, Bob has curtailed his flying stunts and donned a helmet to encourage his followers to do likewise. Bob has not abridged his flying activity, though, and is found in the air more than on the ground. Rumor has it that he is starting to sprout feathers.

Aerodynamicist Irv Culver flies the VJ-23 Swingwing he helped design. This is a rigid-wing, monoplane hang glider distinct from the Rogallo-type. Photo by Downie and Associates.

Dave Muehl of Eipper Formance views a famous sign at Torrance Beach, Calif., one of the early hang glider flying sites. Photo by Downie and Associates.

Irv Culver

My first encounter with Irv Culver was at a seminar on ultra-light flying machines at Northrop Institute of Technology where he spoke about pressure gradients quite knowledgeably. He appears to strangers to be the typical genius with about 60 years of college and then you become aware of the fact that he is a very modest, sincere person. He possesses a sixth sense for recognizing when he loses you in a conversation. Before you have time to ask a question he will completely rephrase his last statement in the clearest terminology.

While speaking on one subject, you sense he is thinking about 15 minutes ahead to the next subject. When talking to him, you feel that you are talking to a computer, except a computer takes longer to answer.

If you asked him what the lift coefficient of a frog is he would probably ask, "What type of frog?"

It wasn't until later that I found out Irv is largely self-educated as an engineer, a virtue few can claim. He is presently working on a new design for a hang glider which he believes will be safer than the present designs. Knowing Irv, it probably will be.

Dave Muehl

I once worked with Dave Muehl, who is now associated with Eipper Formance. He is the type of person who becomes involved not only eight hours a day, but 24 hours a day. That's how involved Dave is in kites. It's not a job any longer, it's his life. I once heard him say that he was donating the rest of his life to the sport. Dave cannot be classified as a natural pilot but he is a dedicated pilot who spends every minute of free time flying, not sitting around on a beach talking about it. Whatever he lacks in natural ability, he makes up for in determination and perseverance. He is now working on a project to give the standard Rogallo better control in turns. Dave can frequently be found at big meets competing for best pilot award. He has contributed much to the sport in the way of safety and knowledge based on his years of experience.

Bill Allen

Bill Allen is responsible for much of the success of the sport due to his talents in the fields of photography and writing. He started working for Eipper Formance as head of their public relations department. Later, as the sport grew, he felt he could do more by working on the United States Hang Gliding Association magazine, *Ground Skimmer*. He soon became editor and the magazine quickly took on its professional appearance. Bill has since gone back to school to further his knowledge in the field of writing. In losing Bill Allen, the sport lost a vital part of its foundation, a part which cannot be replaced, only repaired by time.

Joe Faust

Joe Faust is the editor of a magazine called *Low and Slow*. It was the first magazine in the movement, published in the attic of his home in his spare time. Spare time was when Joe was not studying new designs for kites and flying machines. Joe does not have a lot of friends due to the fact that he prints exactly what he feels in his magazine. Whether right or wrong, he at least takes a stand and voices his opinion. Joe has an uncanny resemblance to Elliot Gould.

Joe is always willing to discuss new ideas and can be reached at his office in Santa Monica at the most ungodly hours. Joe has a different approach to skysurfing than the average flyer. He believes a pilot should be a self-soarer, which he practices by not accepting help carrying or launching his glider. Every flight Joe takes is an experiment which he conducts in his head and later transfers to his magazine. He has flown more different types of gliders than most people have ever seen. Joe has a knack which allows him to become accustomed to a new design just by looking at it or lifting it. When he finally steps off a hill with a new configuration he looks as if he has flown it all his life.

The following people are also actively involved in the sport and, for the benefit of those interested in learning more about certain aspects of it, their names and occupations follow:

Dave Cronk — Designer of the Cronk Kite and Cronk Sail

Bob Lovejoy — Designer of the Quicksilver

Carol Boenish Price — Editor of *Ground Skimmer*

Dave Kilborne — Sport Specialties

Taras Kiceniuk, Jr. — Owner and builder of the Icarus II and V

Chuck Stahl — the USHGA flight director

Dr. Paul MacCready — former international soaring champion

Lloyd Licher — President of USHGA

Volmer Jensen — owner and pilot of the VJ-23 and VJ-24

Kaz De Lisse — Vice President of USHGA

Mike Riggs — owner and designer of the Seagull

Jack Lambie — designed the Hang Loose

Pete Brock — owns Ultralite Products and President of the Hanglider Manufacturers Assn.

12. Terminology

Aerodynamics — the science of air in motion

Air — a blanket of gases surrounding the Earth; a mixture of dense gases, nitrogen and oxygen; air is mobile and readily displaced or set in motion by solid objects or by heating

Aircraft — any machine made for flying whether it be heavier or lighter than air

Airflow — air circulating or flowing freely; a certain direction that air is flowing

Airfoil — an aircraft surface designed to produce reaction from the air

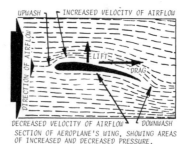

SECTION OF AEROPLANE'S WING, SHOWING AREAS OF INCREASED AND DECREASED PRESSURE.

Airframe — the main structure of an aircraft

Air Resistance — obstruction offered by air to object passing through it

Air Speed — speed at which you travel through the air; not to be confused with ground speed. Example: If you are flying over the ground at 10 m.p.h. into a five m.p.h. wind, your air speed is 15 m.p.h. Or, if you are flying downwind in a 16 m.p.h. wind and your ground speed is 50, you are flying at 34 m.p.h. air speed.

Angle of Attack — angle of an airfoil in relation to the airflow; angle between the line of the normal wind direction and the chord of an airfoil

Apex — point of a triangle or conical object: the apex of a Rogallo is at the nose plate

Biplane — any aircraft having two main wings, one above the other.

Boundary Layer — motionless layer of air next to the surface of the wing which is standing still because of friction

C.G. — center of gravity; the point from which weight is evenly distributed; approximate position where the control bar is connected to the keel; the point at which the glider will balance

Coefficient — any of the factors of a product; a number that serves as a measure

Control Bar — the triangular bar below the airframe which controls the glider; see triangle bar

Density — the ratio of mass to volume

Dive — the nose down attitude of an aircraft in relation to the horizon

Dive Syndrome — the normal tendency for a pilot to want to dive to pick up speed when flying at a high altitude because he has no reference to judge his speed as he has at a low altitude.

Drag — the resistance created by the friction of an object traveling through the air

Dynamic Similarity — the means by which we can predict from measurements made in the wind tunnel on a model airplane the forces which the real airplane will experience

Flow — direction of air over or around an object

Fluid Dynamics — the study of fluids in motion

Flutter — an instability caused by the interaction of air loads with the elasticity and inertia of the structure; commonly confused with flapping. However, flutter does not normally occur when flying slower than the speed of sound

Formulas —

1) $$\text{aspect ratio} = \frac{\text{span}}{\text{average chord}}$$

2) $$\text{average chord} = \frac{\text{span}}{\text{aspect ratio}}$$

3) $$\text{wing loading} = \frac{\text{span}}{\text{total weight}}$$

4) $$\text{Reynolds number} = \frac{\text{density} \times \text{span} \times \text{length}}{\text{viscosity}}$$

Friction — the rubbing of one body against another, as with air against an airfoil

Fuselage — the main body of an aircraft to which the wing and tail are attached

Gravity — force attracting bodies toward center of earth; results in the weight of an object

Hang Glider — (kite, delta wing, Rogallo, flex wing or Porta-Wing) any glider that is foot-launched, weighs less than 150 pounds and is normally folded up for transporting

Glide Ratio — distance an aircraft moves forward in still air while descending a given distance; a glider with a 5:1 (5 to 1) glide ratio will go 5 feet forward for every foot it descends

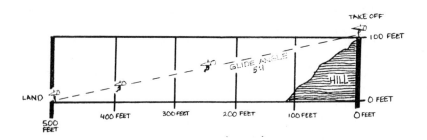

Inertia — the property of matter to remain at rest if at rest, or if moving, to keep moving in the same direction, unless affected by some outside force

Kinetic Theory — the minute particles of all matter are in constant motion and the temperature of a substance is dependent on the velocity of this motion

King Post — vertical post on top of glider from which cables run to four corners of structure to prevent wings from deflecting downward when encountering negative lift

Laminar Airfoils — are made thicker toward the back thus the moving air is made to speed up as it moves across the wing

Laminar Flow — is a very smooth, non-turbulent air flow

Lift — upward force developed from air passing around an airfoil

M.P.A. — man powered aircraft; a glider that uses muscle power instead of an internal combustion engine

Ornithopters — an aircraft designed to be propelled by flapping wings; it never proved practical

Paragliders — paper-dart shaped, metallized fabric kite with leading edge booms, which can be folded away inside a launching rocket during ascent and deployed for re-entry

Parallel Bar — the bottom structure of some hang gliders consisting of two bars running parallel to the keel; structure supporting the pilot in a hanging position

Nose Plate — aluminum or stainless steel part clamping ends of keel and leading edge tubes together; acts as pivot on which to fold the kite

Reynolds Number — is a measure of the ratio of inertial forces to viscous forces; density and viscosity are the fluid properties respectively associated with these forces

Ridge Soaring — extended flight by using vertical air current generated by wind striking side of hill or ridge

Ryan Wings — a family of flexible wing aerial vehicles, an entirely new category of aircraft based on the use of wing surfaces of cloth or other flexible material attached to a keel and leading edge members to form an arrow-shaped, kite-like structure which supports the payload suspended beneath the wing.

ACG (Air Cargo Glider) — The ACG system, which increases several times the normal internal cargo capacity of helicopters, is being studied by the Army. Jeeps, and other small wheeled carriers, have been carried aloft by ACG systems and towed behind helicopters.

PDG (Precision Drop Glider) — The PDG, designed to carry large quantities of priority cargo into areas of limited landing space, has been tested in the United States and abroad. Dropped from fixed wing aircraft or helicopters, the PDG can "home" on a portable ground beacon, or be remotely controlled to a pinpoint landing by the launch aircraft or an operator on the ground. It has successfully landed payloads of up to 300 pounds.

XV-8A Fleep (Utility Cargo Vehicle) — A Flex Wing Aerial Utility Vehicle. The test program included operations from rough, unprepared desert surfaces, and lifting close to 1,000 pound payloads. Short take-off and landing characteristics make this "flying jeep" ideal as a utility vehicle for military units.

PDGS (Precision Delivery Glider System) — Gliders launched from aircraft designed to deliver payloads of 2,000 pounds, utilizing packaging and deployment concepts of Ryan-built inflatable, Flex Wing gliders already demonstrated under controlled flight conditions for wings sized from 10 to 38 feet in length. The advantages to this system include automatic homing or remote guidance, all-weather capability, and ease of maintenance.

Flex Bee (Surveillance Drone) — Designed for launching from forward areas to bring back intelligence photographs of enemy targets that cannot be seen from the launch site. They are ground launched by a portable rail launcher using a cartridge type propellant actuated by a lanyard, and can be maintained and operated by only two men.

TUG (Towed Universal Glider) — Designed to deliver 4,000 pound payloads, the largest payloads ever carried in a Flex Wing vehicle. Cargo body suspended beneath the Flex Wing will be able to carry liquid petroleum or high priority dry cargo, including ammunition, food, machinery and other esential items.

LUG (Light Utility Glider) — Based on the Army's operational requirement for an extremely versatile cargo delivery vehicle of simple design and low cost, urgently needed for use in a highly mobile and dispersed combat environment. Payloads ranging from 1,000 to 5,000 pounds can be suspended beneath it and towed by a rotary wing Army aircraft.

IDG (Individual Drop Glider) — Designed and tested for the Army. Airborne troops can control their direction and rate of descent after jumping from aircraft. When the system is fully developed, airborne personnel using the IDG system could, for example, be released at 10,000 feet altitude approximately seven miles horizontal distance from the target, and glide themselves to a pre-determined objective in controlled descent.

Flex Wing (Manned Test Bed) — Successfully flown in 1961 to demonstrate functional and aerodynamic characteristics. Upon completion of this flight test program, the test bed was presented to the Army who cooperated with NASA in successful completion in the actual test flights.

Saddle — fitting between two crossed aluminum tubes to prevent deformation

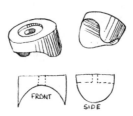

Sails — the shaped sheets of canvas, Dacron or any material stretched over the wing area or made as the wing.

Shear Stress — the action or force causing two contacting parts or layers to slide upon each other, moving apart in opposite directions parallel to the plane of their contact.

Soar — to glide without losing altitude; to rise above the usual or ordinary level

Spin — aircraft dive in a spiral path of large pitch and small radius; can happen when a stall occurs in mid-flight

Stall — when the wing loses lift; this can happen at any speed

Stagnation Point — a point of zero speed; as a fluid particle moves from the stagnation point downstream along an airfoil it accelerates to its maximum speed

Streamline — the shaping of bodies to promote a smooth airflow

Stress — an applied force usually measured in pounds per square inch

Subsonic Speed — speeds that are less than that of sound through air

Surface Area — the area on the surface of the wing

Swaging — process of crimping nico sleeves onto cable

Tang — rectangular piece of metal with a hole on each end to allow a thimble to be attached to a bolt

Tuft — a piece of yarn approximately 6″ long, used to show air flow over a surface

Tension — straining or stretching force

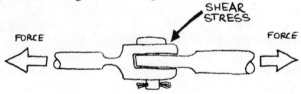

TENSION FORCE

Thermal — column of hot air rising upward creating lift; usually found over black or dark areas which absorb heat more readily

Titanium Tetrachloride — also known as liquid smoke; highly corrosive chemical that combines with water vapor in the air to form dense, fine smoke; smoke is also highly toxic

Triangle Bar (Trapeze Bar) — triangular structure suspended on pivot under Rogallo used by pilot for control by weight shifting; sometimes referred to as the control bar

Vortex — a circular airflow which causes induced drag normally at the wing tip

Wake — the turbulent air left behind by passage of an object; can be dangerous if encountered by a hang glider

Wave Soaring — the continuation of lift behind a hill or obstacle, directly behind a sink area

Wind Tunnel — structure designed for creating a smooth flow of air through a test chamber at controllable speeds for the purposes of testing shapes and flows

13. Technical Notes

At Northrop Institute of Technology, an all-day seminar on hang gliders devoted attention to the structural considerations of hang gliders. Some interesting points were brought out which may help you decide what type of glider to purchase or will give you a good working knowledge of structures.

Basic Structures

A structure is a mechanism designed and built to resist force and carry loads. Any structure can be broken down into three basic elements, the bar, the plate, and the shell. Each of the elements has a level of resistance to stress depending on the type of stress, the level of the load, and the speed at which the load is applied. A basic knowledge of simple structures should be studied by any individual constructing or designing a hang glider.

Let me explain a basic problem you may encounter in the design of a simple high aspect ratio Rogallo. Say you take a standard 90° nose kite and to gain lift you widen the angle to 130° and lengthen the spar to connect to the tips of the leading edges. Now with this high aspect ratio your CL has just jumped to the bow of your new ship and your old C.G. is too far back to get penetration. The structural problem? Can the boom support your weight in a bending load? If not, what structure can replace the boom that would hold the load? Or, how can you turn the bending load to a compression load with the fewest structural elements?

With a basic knowledge of structure, you can design a kite that is light, strong, durable and portable. With this same basic knowledge, you can redesign or avoid any designs that are structurally unsafe!

Computing for Strength

If we can figure the maximum load a structural member will undergo, we can select an alloy that has the right kind of strength for the load, or we can obtain the necessary strength by increasing the cross section dimension of the critical member. This can be achieved by increasing the wall thickness of a tube or the diameter of that tube.

A simple formula to find the tensile strength of a metal structure:

$$\text{TENSILE STRENGTH} = \frac{\text{MAXIMUM LOAD (lb)}}{\text{CROSS SECTIONAL AREA (sq in)}}$$

or if tensile strength is known:

MAXIMUM LOAD (lb) = KNOWN TENSILE STRENGTH (psi) × CROSS SECTIONAL AREA (sq in)

The main reason for knowing the effect of loads is that hang gliding is not regulated by the F.A.A. or any association, so you may be the only one who ever inspects your kite for structural integrity.

One of the problems with the standard Rogallo is that the leading edges have cantilevered wing tips. This is the portion of the leading edge tube that extends about four feet behind the cross tube without any support. This leading edge is subject to two loads, bending and compression, just like a wing spar or beam in a monoplane.

But most monoplane wings use two spars, a front and a rear with a combination of compression tubes, drag wires and anti-drag wires. Also, the spars in a monoplane are designed as beams to take the load better than a tube would. The tube is a poor man's compromise!

Another fact to take into consideration is that a weak spot exists on each leading edge where a vertical hole exists for cross-tube connection.

Larger Tubing

The trend in hang gliding is to use smaller diameter tubing, not larger! I believe this is unwise because if you test the tensile strength of a 1¾″ diameter tube and a 2″ tube of 6061-T6 with a .058″ wall, you will find:

$$1¾″ × .058 = 14,850 \text{ psi}$$
$$2″ × .058 = 18,900 \text{ psi}$$
$$\text{Difference of } 4,050 \text{ psi}$$

Now, let's look at the weight savings to see if it's worth it:

$$1\ 3/3″ × .058 × 18′ = 6.48 \text{ lbs}$$
$$2″ × .058 × 18′ = 7.92 \text{ lbs}$$
$$\text{Difference of } 1.44 \text{ lbs}$$

On a standard kite of four tubes, this would mean a 5.76 lb difference at the price of losing 4,050 p.s.i. tensile strength.

In a hang glider, the seated position is much more comfortable than the prone, but creates more drag. The cables suspending the seat should behind this flyer's shoul-der for safety.

Unlike a monoplane, a Rogallo is seldom inspected, possibly because of its simplicity of design. But every Rogallo flying is developing fatigue from continuous bending of the leading edge tubes. I feel that the main structure should be built of at least 1⅞″ × .058 6061-T6 tubing.

Wing tips are vulnerable, but you can reduce the possibility of an accident by proper sleeving of the leading edge tubes. Wood dowels were used commonly on the earlier Rogallos but they can create another problem by swelling and cracking the tubing if they become wet. The tubing can also shear at the end of the dowel if the dowel is not rounded off. Aluminum sleeves are safer than dowels, if they are the proper diameter and length.

You might consider bracing the tube by extending the cross tube an extra foot and running cables from the nose plate to the cross tube ends and back to the wing tips.

The Whitney Design

You can use the Whitney design, which is a keel and a cross tube with a cable around the perimeter. This provides a cable leading edge with a tension load on it. A 3/32 7 × 19 flexible, carbon cable has a breaking strength of 2,000 and for an 18-foot leading edge weighs .18 lbs.

A ⅛ 7 × 19 flexible, carbon cable has a breaking strength of 2,000 lbs and for an 18-foot leading edge weighs .36 lbs.

As you can see, cable will take the tension with no problem. This puts the cross tubing under a compression load. There are no shear, bending, or torsional loads exerted in this design. It requires less material, it is lighter, and has more lift than a standard Rogallo. And it is also much stronger. I have built and flown this design for over a year and found it to be the solution to the Rogallo problem. Mine weighs 25 lbs.

Whitney Enterprises has protection on design rights to this kite against manufacturers, but welcomes and encourages individuals to build and experiment with this design. Whitney is willing to give any findings to anyone interested.

Other Designs

There are other designs available that offer higher performance but are not as portable as the Rogallo. It seems that the better the performance, the poorer the transportability.

Here are different categories of gliders, listed according to control ability:

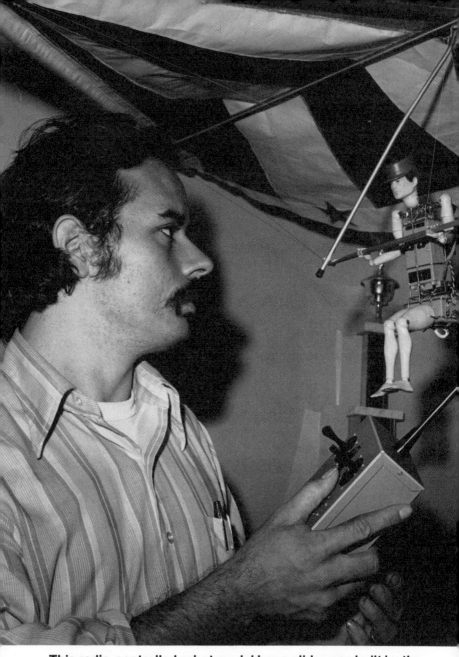

This radio-controlled robot model hang glider was built by the author for testing designs. It works well and gets a lot of attention!

1) Weight shift only
2) Weight shift and control surface
3) Control surface only

In the **weight shift only** you have the standard Rogallo. They have a glide ratio of 1:2 up to 1:3.5. They are of simple construction, can be flown with little skill, and weigh anywhere from 25 lbs to 55 lbs. However, it should be stated that by using a center of gravity shift as the only means of control, the lateral control effectiveness of this system decreases at low angles of attack, where the fabric luffs, and is also decreased at high angles of attack near the stall. N.A.C.A. report TND-2291 reports an unexpected tumbling motion encountered after a stall. After the model was tumbling the control (weight shift) was ineffective to stop the tumble. Severe loads were encountered on the leading edge and cross tube, and in some cases they would fail. In mild, gentle stalls there is little or no tendency to tumble. It should be pointed out that the **weight shift only** type glider should only be flown in mild winds and whip stalls should be avoided.

There is another design in the **weight shift only** class that should be mentioned. It is the para-glider or para-foil, the completely flexible wing with no structure to hold it in the deployed state except the lift of the wind. It must be opened, then pointed into the wind until it lifts itself up. The pilot hangs below the wing on lines forming an acute angle, the pilot being located at the apex of the angle. Pitch is mild so it is hard to get into a bad stall or dive.

The **weight shift and control surface** glider would include some high-aspect ratio Rogallos such as the Cronk kite. It would also include the Chanute type (previously used all weight-shift) biplane, the Icarus II, and Lovejoy's Quicksilver monoplane. In most of these designs, weight shift is used for pitch control. Because of the sensitivity of pitch control, weight seems adequate. However, you do get a loss of sensitivity at extremely high or low angles of attack. They take more skill to fly than the standard Rogallo, some take a small ground crew to help launch and carry, and transporting sometimes requires a truck.

The **control surface only** craft has three-axis control. Examples: the Waterman biplane, the Volmer VJ-11, and the Volmer VJ-23, the last being a cantilevered wing. The VJ-23 is probably the most advanced design to date. It requires about 30 minutes to assemble

Free flight indeed! Perfect form with tucked legs. Skysurfing in its exhilarating element.

and transporting requires a trailer. Although owner claims cost of materials to be about $400, I believe this must be a very low estimate.

Flying Wings

A pure flying wing would be a "flying plank." The secret of stability with the plank configuration is in the airfoil. It must have a considerable amount of reflex. An example: the C.G. must be about 20% when the angle of attack is 6°. Forty per cent of the rear portion of the airfoil is used to obtain stability.

With the swept-back flying wing, you will not need as much reflex for stability. The moment of the wing tip area is further back so that a little reflex goes a long way. Some of the flying wings available today are Taras Kiceniuk, Jr.'s Icarus V, Dave Cronk's Cronk Sail, Richard Miller's Condor, The Colver Skysail, and the Whitney Porta-Plane.

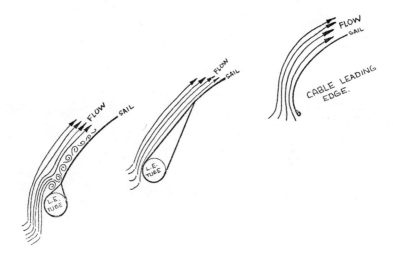

Attaching Sails

Sail application influences structural loads at the leading edge and cross tube connections. If a Dacron sail is used, there is a bending load on the bolt at location between cross tube and leading edge.

The main problem with the plastic sail is that it is installed by taping the plastic to the leading edge tube then rolling the tube 360° and bolting it to the cross tube. Now as lift increases, you get a torsional load on the leading edge tubes (known as a symmetrical system of loads). In a strong up gust, you could overstress the cross tube bolt. So, rolling of the sail should be avoided. I have found that when you roll your sail, you get more lift and your CL is a little farther forward. I believe this is because you get a smoother flow over the top of the sail whereas the pocket created with a Dacron sail induces drag above and just past the L.E. tube where sail is sewn. A possible cure might be to lengthen the L.E. tube pocket for smoother flow.

14. Dealers

Because of the growth of the sport of skysurfing, no dealer list can be complete; it tends to be out of date before it reaches print. There probably are new dealers near you representing various manufacturers who have started in business since this list was compiled. Invariably, too, some of the dealers listed here may have moved or otherwise changed since the list was compiled. Despite these unavoidable deficiencies, it is hoped this list will be useful for obtaining information, buying kits, plans, parts, or complete gliders.

ALASKA

Falcon Air
Jerry Chism
4049 Mallard
Fairbanks, Ak. 99701

Gary King Jr.
308 East Northern Lights
  Blvd.
Anchorage, Ak. 99503
807-272-3118

ARIZONA

Bill Allen
2638 North Champlain
Tempe, Az. 85281
602-945-2514 Home,
602-955-6487 Bus.

Jim Allen — Tim Agersea
6016 East Quartz Mt. Road
Paradise Valley
Phoenix, Az. 85253
Jim — 602-948-0734
Tim — 602-849-6439

Chandelle Phoenix

ARIZONA (cont.)

Ski Haus Action Sports
Charlie Lutz
2501 East Indian School Road
Phoenix, Az.
602-264-1224

Chandelle Tucson
Ski Haus Action Sports
Charlie Lutz
2823 East Speedway
Tucson, Az. 85716
602-881-4544

John Fox
3147 No. 31 Ave.
Phoenix, Az. 85017
602-272-6661 or 602-269-8222

Genesis II, Inc.
John Leathers
P.O. Box 3526
Phoenix, Az. 85030

Dan Gregory (Icarus II)
3319 No. Park
Tucson, Az. 85719

U.S. Hangliders
11024 N. 22nd Avenue 5
Phoenix, Az. 85029
602-944-1655

ARKANSAS
Stanley Newton
P.O. Box 163, Rt. 5
Hot Springs, Ar. 71901

CALIFORNIA
Aeolus
631 Redwood Rd
Bill Armour, Bob Locke
Felton, Ca. 95018
408-335-5798

Boat & Motor Mart
3250 Army St.
San Francisco, Ca. 94110
415-824-3545

Casa De Motor Homes
Ward Low
2605 Wagon Wheel Drive
Oxnard, Ca. 93030
805-485-1818

Chandelle San Francisco
Lee Sterios
2123 Junipero Sierra Blvd.
Daly City, Ca. 94015
415-756-0650

Chandelle Fresno
c/o Alpine Haus
4777 Blackstone
Fresno, Ca. 93726
Dean Paschall
209-229-9591

Chandelle West
17815 Sky Park Blvd. A

Irvine, Ca. 92707
Mike Schlinger
714-979-7413

Dadealus
111 12th Street
Del Mar, Ca.

Escape Country
Jim Robinson
Robinson Ranch
Trabuco Canyon, Ca. 92678
714-586-7964

Falcon Hang Gliding
Don Balch
1121 Burlingame Ave.
Burlingame, Ca. 94010
415-342-2210

Flight Realities
Bob Skinner
1945 Adams Ave.
San Diego, Ca.
714-298-1962

Flight Realities
Steve Huckhert
2414 Park Way
Bakersfield, Ca. 93304
805-323-9759

Free-Flight of San Diego
P.O. Box 15722
San Diego, Ca. 92115

Free-Flight of Manteca
James T. Penny
17810 Kram
Manteca, Ca. 95336

Free-Flight of the Monterey
 Peninsula
2201 Fremont Blvd.

Monterey, Ca. 93940

Free-Flight Systems of
Orange County
1700 Superior Ave.
Costa Mesa, Ca. 92627
714-642-5656

Free-Flight of Fresno
P.O. Box 589
Fresno, Ca. 93208
209-222-8111

Free-Flight of Stockton
1135 Dlivery
Stockton, Ca. 95204

Jim Gree
3726 No. Van Ness Blvd.
Fresno, Ca. 93704
209-222-6025

Mike Green
111 12th St.
Del Mar, Ca.
714-755-3128

Hangliders of California
11545 Sorrento Valley Road
Bldg. 3, Suite 303
San Diego, Ca. 92121
714-452-0351

Hawk Industries
5111 Santa Fe Street
San Diego, Ca. 92109
714-272-7449

J & G Aircraft
1137 Jameston Dr.
Sunnyvale, Ca. 94087
415-948-4524
Bill Johnson
2211 Vera Cruz

Modesto, Ca. 95350
207-521-5289

Dennis Kulberg
43 Panoramic Way
Walnut Creek, Ca. 94595
415-938-0220

Mark Livesay
9489 Mission Park Place
Santee, Ca. 92071
714-449-0343

Manta Livermore
Jeff Johnson, Jamie Adam,
Vinny Salemme
326 Michell Ct.
Livermore, Ca. 94550
415-447-7100

Tic Musser
2842 North Hacienda
Fresno, Ca. 93705
209-227-2282

Don Partridge
P.O. Box 404
Bishop, Ca. 93514
714-873-5070

Dave Rachubka
3121 Coral St.
Morro Bay, Ca. 93442
805-772-3794

Steve Rooney, Jr.
3210 Balmoral Dr.
Sacramento, Ca. 95821
916-489-0476

Ron Rupp
Homewood Resort
P.O. Box 165
Homewood, Ca. 95718

916-525-7256

Jim Rusing
Sea World
1720 South Shores Rd.
San Diego, Ca. 92109
714-222-6363 Ext. 216

Seagull Soaring
P.O. 5474
Carmel, Ca. 93921
408-394-3347

Bruce Shade
4817 Forrestal St.
Fair Oaks, Ca. 95628
916-961-1472

Ray Shannon
512 Jefferson
Bakersfield, Ca. 93305
805-327-2054

Speed & Marine Assoc.
401 W. Chapman
Orange, Ca. 92666

Sunbird Ultralite Gliders
Gary Valley
21420 Chase St., No. 7
Canoga Park, Ca. 91304
213-882-3177

Tahoe Hang Glider
 Specialists
Jim Worral
P.O. Box 2366
Olympic Valley, Ca. 95730
916-582-2700

Ultralite Flying Machine
3008 Lawrence Expressway
Santa Clara, Ca. 95051

Bob Velzy
13077 E. Rosecrans Blvd.
Santa Fe Springs, Ca. 90670
213-921-4111

Volbron Hang-Gliding School
Fritz Braunberger
2465 Bantry Ln.
So. San Francisco, Ca. 94080
415-873-1731

Windways Flying Machines
Mike Turchin
1368 Max Ave.
Chula Vista, Ca. 92011
714-427-8514

William Wooley Jr.
3801 Allen Road
Bakersfield, Ca.
805-589-2555

Windsong
27 North Garden
Ventura, Ca. 93001

COLORADO
Alpine Haus
Joe Decker
628 South College
Fort Collins, Co. 80521
303-482-2043

Free-Flight of Alamosa
George Guerin
3 Bellwood Drive
Alamosa, Co. 81101

Free-Flight of Canon City
Fremont Sales & Service
P.O. Box 70, 1421 So. 9th
Canon City, Co. 81212

Get High, Inc.
P.O. Box 4551
Aspen, Co. 81611
John Totman
303-925-3275

Gorsuch, Ltd.
Dave Gorsuch
P.O. Box 1508
Vail, Co. 81657
303-925-3275

Country Bicycle Works
701 West Hampden Ave.
Cinderella City
Englewood, Co. 80110
John Getz
303-761-6113

C.B. Jensen Serna Group
c/o J.L.S. Flying Service
Box 22
Hideaway Park, Co. 90540
303-726-5969

Life Cycle
Bill Snyder, Tom Palmer
1224 15th Street
Denver, Co. 80202
303-572-8405

Naturally High Flight
 Systems
P.O. Box 5218
Steamboat Spring, Co.
 80499
Anthony Matthews

Rocky Mountain Marine
Dos Chappel, Gurney Munn
5421 Leetsdale Dr.
Denver, Co. 80222

Sun Sail Corp.
Ted Schmiedeke
6753 E. 47th Ave. Dr.
Denver, Co. 80216
303-321-8482

Werners Storm Hut
Hand Edwards
Steamboat Springs, Co.
 80477

CONNECTICUT
Lee Keeler
Purchase Hill
Southbury, Ct. 06488
203-354-7231

FLORIDA
Jerry H. Blount
804 Poinciana Dr.
Gulf Breeze, Fl. 32561
904-932-4138

Hal Elgin's Holiday Water
 Sports
6639 Emerson Ave. South
St. Petersburg, Fl. 33707
813-345-3697

Island Park Bayfront
Don. R. Hill
P.O. Box 2868
Sarasota, Fl. 33578
813-366-6659

Jerry Hogan
360 South Highway 19
Crystal River, Fl. 32629
904-795-4736 or 795-2496

GEORGIA
Appalachian Mountaineering

5725 Buford Highway N.E.
Atlanta, Ga. 30340

B & H Sales
John Burford
349 N. Four Lane Hiway
Marietta, Ga.
404-428-0037

WDM Enterprises
William D. McDonald
2770 Burfordi Dr.
Marietta, Ga. 30060

Jimmy Spears
128 Reynolds St.
Agusta, Ga. 30901
404-738-7415

HAWAII

Air Performance
Paul Bates & Bob Thornburg
217 Prospect
Honolulu, Hi. 96813
808-524-3084

Mike Dorn
5283 Kalanianaole Hwy.
Honolulu, Hi. 96821

John Hughs
P.O. Box 337
Lawai, Kauai Hi. 96765

Manta Hawaii
Michel Downing
762 So. Queen St.
Honolulu, Hi. 96813

Stan Truitt
P.O. Box 7, Kula
Maui, Hi. 96790

IDAHO

Chandelle Idaho
Bob Ware
P.O. Box 1221
Sun Valley, Id. 83353
208-726-4843

Free-Flight of Twin Falls
259 Main Ave. E.
Twin Falls, Id. 83301

Mike Hester
3051 Rowland Lane
Boise, Id. 83703
203-342-8635

Jones Brothers
Larry & Windle
2901 State St.
Boise, Id. 83702
208-344-7774

Millers Marina & Pro Shop
1710 So. Roosevelt St.
Boise, Id. 83705
208-343-2830

Pegasus
Bob Baldeck
636 5th Ave.
Lewiston, Id. 83501

Soaring Sports
Box 2764
Idaho Falls, Id. 83401
208-523-1677

Sun Valley Kite School
Jerry Miller, Director
Sun Valley, Id.
208-622-3511

ILLINOIS

Apollo Skysailing Centers
Dave Koch

722 Barrington Rd.
Streamwood, Il. 60103
312-289-5313

Chandelle Chicago
Dave Snook
109 West Prospect
Mt. Prospect, Il. 60056
312-398-3451

Ben Heck
Bennetts
7191 West Grand
Chicago, Il. 60635
312-637-1007 or 672-1206

Arthur R. Koch
9702 Shore Dr.
Rockford, Il. 61111
815-654-0080

Harold W. Lewis
139 South Center St.
East Alton, Il. 62024
618-259-4737

Munson Marine Inc.
Box 538, RFD 1
Round Lake, Il. 60073
815-385-2720

IOWA
Boag Chumbley
8219 Lista Lane & 1323 Park
 Ave.
Des Moines, Ia. 50315
515-285-8594

Stanley E. Samuelson
Oscella, Ia.
515-342-2789

KANSAS
Peter Hadley

6901 West 194th
Stillwell, Ks. 66085
913-432-4766

Benny Jumper
Country Estates 12B
Kays, Ks. 67601
913-625-7576

D.W. Kite Sales & Service
Harold Steves
200 West 30th, Suite 102
Topeka, Ks. 66611
913-266-8755

KENTUCKY
Ron Oakley
8400 Blue Lick Road
Louisville, Ky. 40219
502-969-6295

Buel Stalls, Jr.
P.O. Box 69
Murray, Ky. 42071
502-753-3474 or 753-8207

LOUISIANA
Ark-La-Tek Divers Supply
Paul Oberle
9118 Blom
Shreveport, La. 71108

Charles Elmer
Herman J. Salzer
7902 Breakwater Dr.
New Orleans, La. 70124
504-885-0449 or 288-3633

MAINE
Free-Flight of Bangor
Snoops Sales
63 Union Street
Bangor, Me. 04401

Paul Laliberte
Star Route
Kingsfield, Me. 04947 &
Box 142
Biddeford, Me. 04005
207-282-5531

MARYLAND
James M. Krauk
8023 Yellowstone Rd.
Kingsville, Md. 21087
301-592-2233

MICHIGAN
Foot Launch Flyers
2597 Kingstowne Dr.
Walled Lake, Mi. 48088
313-285-6960

Free-Flight of Ann Arbor
8778 Main St.
Whitmore Lake, Mi. 48189

Free-Flight of Grand Rapids
Gar's Sports Center
2531 S. Division Ave.
Grand Rapids, Mi. 49507

Rudolph Kishazy
1460 Junction, Apt. 3
Plymouth, Mi. 48170
313-455-7920

Jim Laure
1441 Spruce Dr.
Kalamazoo, Mi. 49001
616-327-3075

Sky Sails of Michigan
1611 St. Woodward
Royal Oak, Mi. 48067
313-545-0051

Ron Watson

Prime Time Products, Inc.
Box 244
Sarmac, Mi. 48881

John Wessland
Custom Displays
1530 Monroe Ave. NW
Grand Rapids, Mi. 49505
616-364-4510

MINNESOTA
Arrow Marine
Hiway 14 West & 7th St. NW
Rochester, Mn. 55901

Free-Flight of St. Paul
Norcat Inc.
2210 Whitebear
Maplewood, Mn. 55109

Chris Mornes
Mornes, Inc.
1022 West Fourth St.
Grand Rapids, Mn. 55744
218-326-3495

Midwest Sports Center
John Silker
Fairmont, Mn. 56031

Northwestern Hangliders,
 Inc.
212 - 15th Ave. So.
Minn., Mn. 55404
612-333-1771

Fred Tiemens
1215 Washington Ave. So.
Minneapolis, Mn. 55404

MISSISSIPPI
R.B. Prichard
330 Foster Park
Bonneville, Ms. 38829

MISSISSIPPI (cont.)
601-728-5957

MONTANA
Crown Enterprises
Jerry Sanderson
40 East Idaho St.
Kalispell, Mt. 59901
406-756-9377

Free-Flight of Billings
221 Jackson St.
Billings, Mt.
248-6717

Free-Flight of Helena
718 Broadway
Helena, Mt. 59601

Free-Flight of Moorhead
The Escape Hatch
1815 No. 11th St.
Moorhead, Mt. 56560

Free-Flight of Poplar
Monte Martin
Box 35
Poplar, Mt. 59255

Bill Johnson
P.O. Box 2009
Missoula, Mt. 59801
406-549-5076

George V. Nilson, NFT Inc.
P.O. Box 2367
Great Falls, Mt.
406-453-2404

NEBRASKA
 Buzz's Body Shop & Marine
 Supply
R.R. Ave. E, P.O. Box 72
Kearney, Nb. 68847
402-237-2624

NEBRASKA (cont.)
City Lock & Marine
Pat Conrad
2031 St. Marys Ave.
Omaha, Nb. 68102
402-341-9672

Midwest Free-Flight
P.O. Box 205
Fairfield, Nb. 68938

NEVADA
Wings
Bill Duca
318 E. Hoover
Las Vegas, Nv. 89105

Sierra Wings
890 So. Main St.
Falon, Nv. 89406
702-423-4544

Sierra Wings
253 E. Arroyo St.
Reno, Nv. 89502
825-7740

NEW JERSEY
Action Sport Cycles
108 Essex Ave.
Metuchen, NJ 08440
201-494-5555

Delta Wing East
Bernie Yaged
Box 74
Holmdel, NJ
201-542-8535

Free-Flight of Lebanon
Antonio A. Nicorvo
1 Lynwood Dr.
Lebanon, NJ 08833

Lighter Than Air Products

113

40 Center St.
Springfield, NJ 07081
201-467-3562

Joe Mironov
876 Red Rd.
Teaneck, NJ 07666
201-836-9210

NEW MEXICO
Base Camp
Peter Hayes
121 West San Francisco St.
Santa Fe, NM 87501
505-982-9707

Danny King
Box 877
Deming, NM 88030
505-546-5738

Larry Newman
1825 1 Mary Ellen, N.E.
Albuquerque, NM 87108

New Mexico Sky Sails
Don Marshall
625 Amherst N.E.
Albuquerque, NM 87106
505-299-8322

Sky Sailors, Sales & Service
7208 Arroyo Del Dro NE
Albuquerque, NM 87109

NEW YORK
Tim Eldridge
P.O. Box 42
Oneonta, NY 13820
607-432-8483 after 5

Free-Flight of Buffalo
3973 Harlam
Snyder, NY

Free-Flight of Buffalo
Michael Brennan
364 No. Ivyhurst Rd.
Buffalo, NY 14226

Free-Flight of Fayetteville
David Deming
Hoag Lane
Fayetteville, NY 13066

Free-Flight of Herkiner
Mark J. Senit
Herkiner, NY 13350

Free-Flight of Hicksville
Vincent Matassa
77 East End Ave.
Hicksville, Long Island, NY
  11801

Go Fly A Kite Store
1613 - 2nd Ave.
New York, NY 10028
212-988-8885

Fuji Industries Corp.
26 Broadway
New York, NY 10004
212-943-4435

David Montrois
Box 441
Brownsville, NY 13615
315-341-5062

Dick Reynolds
R.D. 1 Upper East St.
Oneonta, NY 13820
607-432-5418

Dan Chapman
Box 57, Ridge Rd.
Marlboro, NY 12542

NORTH CAROLINA

Doss & Sons
434 Brookstown Ave.
Winston-Salem, NC

Free-Flight of Greensboro
Frank J. Howard
2300 Phoenix Dr.
Greensboro, NC 27406

Kitty Hawk Kites
Jockey Ridge
Route 158, P.O. Box 386
Nags Head, NC 27959
919-441-6247

Patton Motor Homes, Inc.
4809 Wilkinson Blvd.
Charlotte, NC 29208

NORTH DAKOTA

John F. Rademacher
101 - 2nd St. South
Fargo, ND 58102

OREGON

Billy B. Beanway Flying
Machine Co.
P.O. Box 22524
Milwaukee, Or. 9722
4217 Railroad Ave. (Shipping
   only)
503-654-8530

C & D Sports
P.O. Box 52
Baker, Or. 97814
503-523-5183

Free-Flight of Corvallis
Dennis Matchette
P.O. Box N
Corvallis, Or. 97330
503-752-9036

OREGON (cont.)

John Ford
312 NE 84th Ave.
Portland, Or. 97220
503-253-6631

Hanggliders Northwest
312 NE 84th
Portland, Or. 97220
503-253-6631

Pacific Hanggliders
Mike Moore
1729 Labona Dr.
Eugene, Or. 97401
503-484-9900

Pacific Hanggliders
1180 West 2nd
Eugene, Or. 97402
484-9900

Southern Oregon Marina
P.O. Box 37
Phoenix, Or. 97535
503-535-2396

OHIO

Chuck's Glider Supplies
2700 Royalton Rd.
Columbia Station, Oh. 44028
216-236-8440

Donald Boor
60 Woodland Ave.
Masury, Oh. 44438

Free-Flight of Mansfield
2429 Pavonia Rd.
Mansfield, Oh. 44903

Ross Strayer
742 Park View Dr.
Wauseon, Oh. 43567

PENNSYLVANIA

Free-FLIGHT OF Greensburg
Log Cabin Wholesale Tire
R.D. 1
Greensburg, Pa.
523-3788

Free-Flight of Reading
620 Walnut St.
Reading, Pa. 19601

Lancaster County Marine
Route 222, 4 Lauber Rd.
Akron, Pa. 17501
717-859-1121

Richard Wilson
6052 Dalmation Dr.
Bethel Park, Pa. 15102

TENNESSEE

Raymond Garner
4431 Namur Grove
Memphis, Tn. 38109

TEXAS

Douglas Baxter
6460 Regal St.
El Paso, Tx. 79904

Steven Lane Branson
8718 Dale Valley
San Antonio, Tx. 78228
Home 512-675-0786
Bus. 512-CA5-7411

Free-Flight of Corpus Christi
Dockside, 315 Beach St.
Box 772
Port Aransas, Tx. 78373
512-749-6141

Free-Flight of Temple
American Handicrafts
719 South 25th St.

Temple, Tx. 76501

Jack Hinson
5206 Greenville Ave.
Dallas, Tx. 75206

Houston Delta Wing
George P. Lasko, Jr.
10614 Plainfield Rd.
Houston, Tx. 77071
713-772-8619

Lauden Aerial
Fred Lauden
2120 South Post Oak
Houston, Tx. 77027
713-627-3613

David O'Neal
2118 70th
Lubbock, Tx. 79412
806-744-2121

Sky Sails, Inc.
3430 Dalworth
Arlington, Tx. 76011
817-261-2556

UTAH

Chandelle Utah
c/o Lift House
3698 E. 7000 S.
Salt Lake City, Ut. 84121
Mike Pogliano
801-277-3944, 363-1498,
272-4236

Free-Flight of Salt Lake
6073 South 530 West
Murray, Ut. 84107

Miller Ski & Cycle Haus
834 Washington Blvd.
Ogden, Ut. 94404

801-392-3911

Robertson Marine
Son Robertson
97 So. Mains St.
Springville, Ut. 84663

Sunset Sports Center
2909 Washington Blvd.
Ogden, Ut. 84401
801-621-2261

Tom Vayada
3209 Imperial St.
Salt Lake City, Ut. 84106
801-487-3586

VERMONT
Trac & Trail Supply, Inc.
Route 107
Gaysville, Vt. 05746
802-234-9684

VIRGINIA
Larry F. Davis
Route 6, Box 36
Martinsville, Va. 24112
703-632-4421

Dave Gibson
823 Pepper Ave.
Richmond, Va. 23226
804-285-4095

Kitty Hawk Kites, Inc.
Tom Powers & John Harris
309 E. Gilpin Ave.
Norfolk, Va. 23503
804-588-4223

Frederic A. Munson
Smith Mountain Dock Inc.
Penhook, Va. 24137
703-927-5100

Max Tufts, Jr.
P.O. Box 166
Warrenton, Va. 22186
203-347-1376

WASHINGTON
Jerry Bain
309 North 19th St.
Kelso, Wa. 98626
206-425-5211

Bruce Barr
17360 Beach Dr. Northeast
Seattle, Wa. 98155
206-363-0900

Bob Bird
Box 7400
Spokane, Wa. 99207

Chandelle Northwest
Ken Greenwald
P.O. Box 4027
Seattle, Wa. 98105
206-682-4655

Delta Wing Kites, Inc.
Bill Joplin & Pete Rutherford
20928 - 133rd S.E.
Monroe, Wa. 98272
206-794-6540

Eastside Boats
Andre Laviqueure
Box 176
Duvall, Wa. 98019
206-788-1002

George Gregor
1425 Marshall
Richland, Wa. 99325
509-943-3951

H & H Water Sports, Inc.

1006 South 198th Pl.
Seattle, Wa. 98148
206-824-2668

Hang Ups, Inc.
Vern Roundtree
30003 112th SE
Auburn, Wa. 98002
206-833-3003

Harley Lester
4914 Ash St.
Spokane, Wa. 99208
509-328-3796

Pegasus
Harley D. Lester
7322 Division St.
Spokane, Wa. 99208
509-484-3822

Pete Rutherford
417 Harvard Ave. East No. 4
Seattle, Wa. 91102
206-322-7190

WISCONSIN
Tommy Bartlett Water
 Shows
P.O. Box 65
Wisconsin Dells, Wi. 53965
608-253-3031

Free-Flight of Watertown
Geogoire Specialties
857 Silver Lake St.
Oconomowoc, Wi. 53066
414-567-2093
Don J. Krueger
8620 W. Auer
Milwaukee, Wi. 53222
414-442-9152

H.H. Petrie Sporting Goods

Mark L. Langenfeld
P.O. Box 5427
Madison, Wi. 53705
608-256-1347

WYOMING
Ken Bird
Box 65
Shoshonie, Wy. 82649

AUSTRIA
Dieter Schulse
Ahamer Strabe 29, A-4800
 Attnang
Puchhaim, Austria

CANADA
Birdman Enterprises
10805 - 73 Avenue, Edmonton
Alberta, T6E 1C8, Canada
403-466-5370

Bob Conners
5711 Blue Bell
West Vancouver, B.C.

Barrie Howie
Box 11
Invermere, B.C. Canada
604-342-9415

Big White Ski Development
R.R. 3 Hall Road
Kelowna, B.C. Canada
604-762-0402

Delta Wing Displays
Bob Jones
Box 892
Kelowna, B.C.

Free-Flight of Midland
Midland Mike's Spec. Sports
P.O. Box 614

Midland, Ontario, Canada

Kitslinno Marine & Lumber
Ltd.
1502 West 2nd Ave.
Vancouver, B.C. Canada
604-736-0166

Mesle Canada, Reg'g.
Joseph A. Messner
Box 610, R.R. 5
Ottawa, Ontario, K1G 3N3
  Canada

R.S. Woyna
20 Cloverdale Crescent
Winnipeg, Manitoba R2C,
  1Z1, Canada
204-222-2949

ECUADOR
Free-Flight of Ecuador
Titan Cia. Limited
10 De Agosto
608 of 25 Casilla 3140
Quito, Ecuador

ENGLAND
Critchley & Hughes
20 Wendover Drive
Fremley, Camberley
Surrey, England

Hi Kites
David Walling
20 Aldsworth Close
Fairford Glso. GL7-4Lb,
  England

FRANCE
Micheal Wyer (Champfort
  Sport)
Route Du Mont'd Arbois
74120 Megue, France

GERMANY
Mike Harker
Postfach 123
81 Garmisch-P, Germany

Volker Mittelmann
5928 Laasphe Bahnhofstr 103
West Germany

GUATEMALA
Almacenes Concordia
C. UBICO & CIA & A
  Ave. Y 18
Calle Zona 1, Guatemela,
  C.A.

JAPAN
Dodge & S Seymour
New Tokyo Blg.
13011 5 Chome
Ginza, Chuo-Ku
Tokyo 104, Japan

Free-Flight of Japan
4-2-3 Chuo
Nakanoku, Tokyo, Japan

MEXICO
Manuel Santos
Papalotes Trepuladas De
  Mexico
Apartado Postal No. 6-731
Mexico 6 D.F., 5 54 21 72

NEW ZEALAND
Pacific Kites, Ltd.
P.O. Box 45-087 Te Atatu
Auckland 8, New Zealand

SWITZERLAND
Chandelle Europa A.G.
Roger Staub
Post Fach 26
8640 Rapperswil, Switzerland
055-276-375

SWITZERLAND (cont.)

Felix Zbinden
Dort 19
1711 Plasselb, Switzerland